PRACTICAL STRATEGIC PLANNING

Practical Strategic Planning

A Guide and Manual for Line Managers

WILLIAM P. ANTHONY

Q

Quorum Books
Westport, Connecticut • London, England

To my family.

Library of Congress Cataloging in Publication Data

Anthony, William P.
 Practical strategic planning.

 Bibliography: p.
 Includes index.
 1. Strategic planning. I. Title.
HD30.28.A54 1986   658.4′012   85–9489
ISBN 0–89930–102–9 (lib. bdg.: alk. paper)

Library of Congress Catalog Card Number: 85–9489
ISBN: 0–89930–102–9

First published in 1985 by Quorum Books

Greenwood Press
A division of Congressional Information Service, Inc.
88 Post Road West, Westport, Connecticut 06881

Printed in the United States of America

The paper used in this book complies with the
Permanent Paper Standard issued by the National
Information Standards Organization (Z39.48–1984).

10 9 8 7 6 5 4 3 2 1

Contents

Exhibits   vii
Preface   xi

PART I   THE BASIC STEPS IN STRATEGIC PLANNING   1

    1. What Is Strategic Planning?   3

    2. How Should Strategic Planning Be Carried Out?   12

    3. Environmental Analysis: Status Quo   25

    4. Environmental Forecast   41

    5. Customer/Market Analysis   49

    6. Strategic Planning Premises and Assumptions   58

    7. Internal Assessment   62

    8. Mission Development   75

    9. Strategic Thrusts or Key Goals   79

PART II   OPERATIONALIZING THE STRATEGIC PLAN   83

    10. Developing and Writing Objectives   85

    11. Developing Action Steps and Schedules   97

    12. Tying to the Budget   123

    13. Tracking, Measuring, and Standards   128

    14. Systems for Corrective Action   132

PART III   AN EXAMPLE OF STRATEGIC PLANNING   145

    15. The Strategic Plan of Spina's Food   147

PART IV APPENDICES   171

    A. Strategic Planning Questionnaire for
       Organizational Assessment   173

    B. Florida Power and Light Economic Forecast   179

Bibliography   199
Index   213

Exhibits

1 The Strategic Planning Process   5

2 Scoping the Outside Environment   27

3 Environmental Assessment   33

4 Worksheet for Environmental Analysis   35

5 Worksheet for Environmental Opportunities and Constraints   37

6 Worksheet for Identifying Correlation and Intensity of Constituent Interest   38

7 Worksheet for Issues Alert System Matrix to Prioritize Environmental Issues   39

8 Worksheet for Completing an Environmental Forecast   43

9 Sample Forecast for Modular Home Manufacturer   45

10 Worksheet Form for Customer Analysis   52

11 Planning Premises for a Municipal Hospital   59

12 Worksheet for Planning Premises   60

13 Worksheet for Internal Assessment   64

14 Worksheet Questions for Survey Feedback Instrument in Smaller Organizations   66

15 Worksheet Questions for Survey Feedback Instrument in Larger Organizations   67

16 The Boston Consulting Group Portfolio Matrix for Classifying Products/Services   69

17 Ratios for Financial Analysis   72

18 Sample Financial Statements for Ratio Analysis   73

19 Sample Mission Statements   77
20 Worksheet for Developing a Mission Statement   78
21 Examples of Strategic Thrusts   80
22 Operationalizing the Strategic Plan   86
23 Criteria for a Good Objective   89
24 Worksheet for Quantifying Hard to Quantify Objectives   89
25 Sample Objectives and Strategic Thrusts   90
26 Worksheet for Writing Objectives   92
27 Worksheet to Set Priorities Using Paired Comparison
   Technique   95
28 Sample Decision Tree   101
29 Optimistic-Pessimistic Scheduling to Determine Realistic
   Time   104
30 Gantt or Bar Chart for Scheduling   106
31 Worksheet Form for Gantt or Bar Chart for Scheduling   107
32 Simplified PERT Diagram of Merger between Two
   Organizational Units   109
33 Worksheet for Tie-In of Objectives   110
34 Sample Worksheet for Tie-In of Objectives   112
35 Worksheet for Tying in Objectives with Key Action Steps   114
36 Sample Worksheet for Tying in Objectives with Action
   Steps   115
37 Time Log and Evaluation Sheet   117
38 Analyzing Your Time Audit   118
39 Leading Time Wasters   118
40 Managing Telephone Calls   119
41 Managing Office Visits   120
42 Twenty Questions for Delegation   121
43 Worksheet for Building Budget Around Objectives   125
44 Sample Budgeting Tie-in Sheet   126
45 Tie-in Sheet for Standards   131
46 Worksheet Form for Corrective Action   137
47 Sample Completed Corrective Action Worksheet   138
48 Worksheet Form for Analyzing Problems   140
49 Spina's Environmental Analysis   151
50 Customer Profile   155

51 Internal Assessment: Strengths and Weaknesses of Spina's 157
52 Action Step Tie-in Worksheet for Restaurant Opening Objective 161
53 Gantt (Bar) Chart for New Restaurant Openings 162
54 Action Step Tie-in Worksheet for Adding New Food Items at Plant 163
55 PERT Chart for New Food Items 164
56 Budgeting Tie-in Sheet for Restaurant Openings 165
57 Budgeting Tie-in Sheet for Producing New Food Items 166

Preface

Strategic planning has been with us for a number of years. Quite a few companies do a good job with the process; others do not. There exists a substantial body of information that can help managers do a better job with strategic planning. Much of this information is not easily available and highly academic in nature.

The purpose of this manual is to present current thinking and research on strategic planning in a usable, readable, and practical form for busy top line executives. Perhaps top executives perform no other role as important as strategic planning, yet many find the process very difficult.

This book is based on a number of years of consulting with a wide variety of business and governmental organizations. It includes techniques I have used successfully in helping organizations develop strategic plans. Since I also teach and do research on the subject in an academic environment, the techniques are solidly grounded in the latest academic writings and research. An annotated bibliography is provided at the end of the book for those who wish more information on particular topics in strategic planning.

The book also contains two other essential ingredients I've found that make the strategic planning process successful. Over 25 forms are presented, both uncompleted and completed with examples that are helpful for planning purposes. A good form can be very useful for synthesizing, recording, and presenting critical information related to a facet of the planning process. The exhibits often replicate the forms and worksheets that managers will find useful to prepare themselves when writing a plan. Please feel free to duplicate any of these forms as needed. No permission is needed.

Secondly, the book contains a complete example of a strategic plan for a company. The plan is based on a real company even though the name, location, and a few other identifying characteristics have been changed to protect the confidentiality of the firm. I've found that organizations unfamiliar with strategic planning not only want to see examples of the various forms used, but also want to see an example of a complete plan.

The strategic planning method presented in this manual is not the only one in existence, but it is one of the best ones from a workability standpoint. It recognizes that strategic planning is a line management responsibility, not something that can be completely delegated to a staff group. It has helped many managers do a better job with strategic planning and I hope it will help you and your organization.

Many thanks to Diane Dyer who typed the manuscript, Eric Valentine who encouraged the project, and Beth Roberts who oversaw the production of the manuscript.

Part I

The Basic Steps in Strategic Planning

The first part of the book addresses the essential steps in the strategic planning process. Beginning with an overview of the strategic planning process, the first chapter reveals why this process is so important in today's organizations. The various ways strategic planning can be carried out are examined in the next chapter.

The basis of strategic planning rests on a thorough understanding of the market. Chapter 3 discusses environmental analysis, which is the first step in planning. The following chapter extends this analysis into the future with an environmental forecast. The customer/market analysis is examined in chapter 5.

Chapter 6 explains how to develop strategic planning premises and key assumptions upon which a strategic plan will be based. In the following chapter, the discussion turns to how an assessment of organizational strengths and weaknesses should be conducted. Chapter 8 shows how to develop a role and mission statement, which provides the basic direction for an organization.

The last chapter in this section reviews how to write strategic thrusts or key goals. These are major targets to achieve during the planning period.

1.

What Is Strategic Planning?

Planning is an essential function for every manager. The old saying, "If you don't know where you're going, any road will take you there," indicates the importance of planning. Without planning, it does not really matter what we do, as the above saying implies. Every path is equally valid since we do not know where we are going.

HOW DOES STRATEGIC PLANNING DIFFER FROM REGULAR PLANNING?

Few managers would disagree with the importance of planning, although they probably would argue that they do not have enough time to do as much planning as they would like. Planning is simply deciding where you want to go and how you want to get there. There are two basic elements to any plan: deciding on a goal or objective and deciding on the best way to reach it.

Most managers do some planning. However, it is usually day-to-day operational planning. In fact, it might be more appropriately called scheduling since the focus is often on a list of activities to be accomplished in a given day or week. The type of planning we discuss in this manual is much different from this. Everyday planning is a part of our discussion but only a small part. Rather, we are concerned with strategic planning. This is substantially different from regular planning as it is often practiced. It differs in importance, scope, resource commitment, time frame, and purpose.

WHAT ARE THE ESSENTIAL ELEMENTS OF STRATEGIC PLANNING?

Strategic planning involves making strategic decisions about major plans for the organization. There are five key elements of strategic planning as follows:

- It recognizes the outside environment and explicitly incorporates elements of it into the planning process.

- It has a long-term time focus, often 3 to 5 years, but sometimes as many as 10 to 20 years.

- It is conducted at the top of the organization and at the top of the organization's major divisions or product groups.

- It involves making decisions that commit large amounts of organizational resources.

- It sets the direction for the organization by focusing on the organization's identity and its place in a changing environment.

Strategic planning serves as the ultimate basis for all that the organization does. It provides the criteria for major investment decisions, such as opening a new plant, for new product/service development, and for budgetary allocation. It also serves as the basis to evaluate the performance of the organization and its managers.

The basic steps in the strategic planning process are shown in Exhibit 1. Even though other models have been proposed and are in use, I've found this one to be the best in terms of completeness and ease of implementation based on a number of years of consulting with a wide variety of business and governmental organizations. Let's briefly look at each of the steps in this model.

Environmental Analysis. The first step to developing a strategic plan is to examine the outside environment surrounding the organization. The idea is to do a point-in-time analysis of significant aspects of the outside environment as they affect the organization. We discuss this step in Chapter 3 of this manual.

Environmental Forecast. After the above step is completed, we now are concerned with predicting how this environment is changing. Trends are explored and new issues of impact are identified. Implications for the future of the organization are explored. We discuss this in Chapter 4.

Customer/Market Analysis. The focus for the reason why the organization exits (i.e., to serve a market) is the next step in the planning process. Emphasis is placed on analyzing how the market is changing and a customer profile of tomorrow is developed. This is discussed in Chapter 5.

Strategic Planning Premises. These reflect key assumptions made about the future. They are based on the forecast and serve as the basis for developing the strategic plan. This is discussed in Chapter 6.

Internal Assessment. We have to establish a planning base and that is the focus here. In this step, we attempt to determine the strengths and weaknesses of the organization as it now exists. Chapter 7 explores this process.

Exhibit 1
The Strategic Planning Process

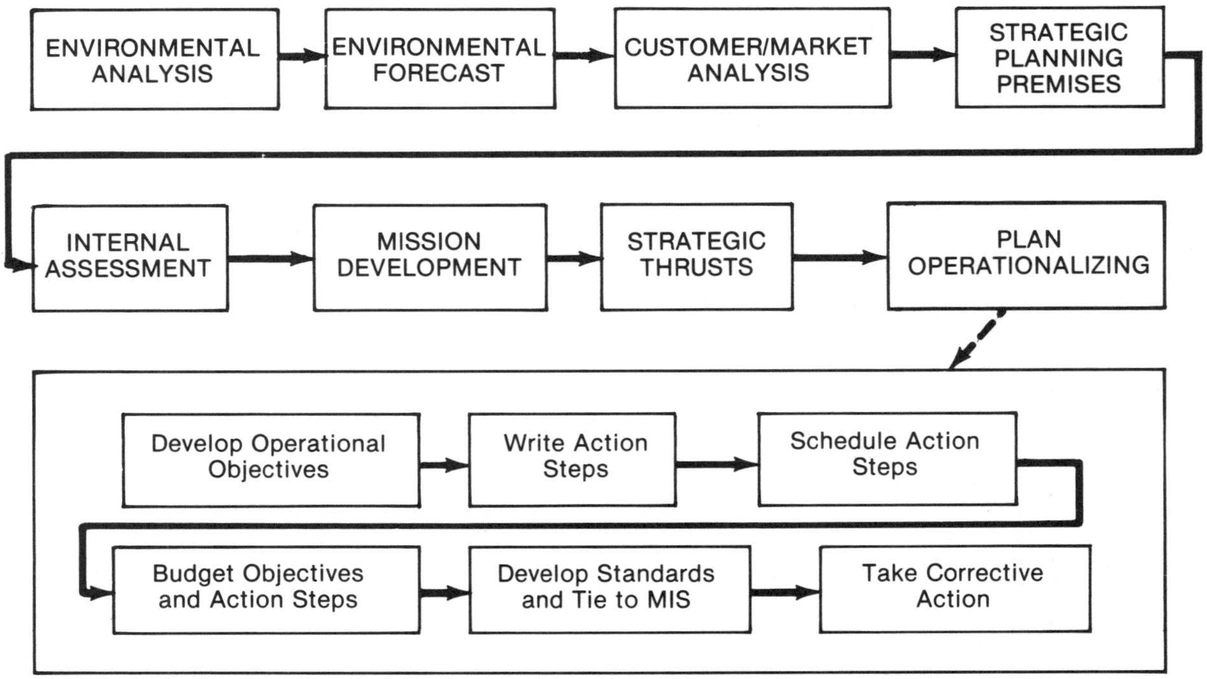

Mission Development. This step in the planning process outlines the role and mission of the organization in view of the environment it faces and the resources it has or can reasonably expect to obtain. The mission provides the ultimate rationale for the organization's existence. It gives the organization identity. Mission development is discussed in Chapter 8.

Strategic Thrusts. These are the three or four major areas where the organization plans to focus its efforts in the next three to five years. They reflect the mission and the forecast. Developing strategic thrusts is discussed in Chapter 9.

Plan Operationalizing. The way to implement the strategic plan, from the development of operational objectives through the process of taking corrective action, is explored in Chapters 10–14 of the manual.

Even though we present the strategic planning process in this step-by-step process, in reality it is not this simple. Even though it is best to proceed in the order suggested here, most organizations will revisit previous steps as it moves through the process. This is good and it emphasizes the need to make the planning process flexible. So many organizations are reluctant to do strategic planning because they fear that once the plans are typed up they are cast in concrete. Managers in these organizations fear that their feet will be held to the fire no matter what happens, so they either refuse to plan or keep their plans vague. This is wrong and a flexible planning process will help avoid this syndrome. (This and other barriers to effective strategic planning are discussed at the end of the next chapter and elsewhere in this book.)

HOW DOES STRATEGIC PLANNING COMPARE TO MBO?

In an organization that uses a comprehensive management by objectives (MBO) system there may be little difference. But since there are several versions of MBO used today, there can be a substantial difference between strategic planning and MBO. The basic difference deals with the breadth and scope of the planning process. In general, MBO tends to be narrower in scope and to deal with the more operational aspects of planning. Often, explicit recognition of the environment never gets fully implemented in the MBO process. Also, MBO tends to focus on a shorter time frame. In our model, MBO is similar to the final step of the strategic planning process—plan operationalizing.

Thus, MBO does have a part to play in strategic planning and a good strategic plan will use the MBO process to operationalize the plan. Consequently, it is important for managers who engage in strategic planning to know how to use MBO. The essential elements of MBO and how it relates to strategic planning are discussed in Chapter 10.

HOW IS STRATEGIC PLANNING RELATED TO
STRATEGIC DECISION MAKING?

When we formulate a strategic plan we are making strategic decisions about the organization. Sometimes, managers tend to view planning and decision making as two separate activities. However, when we plan we make decisions about where the organization is going. We choose among alternative courses of action. We allocate resources in order to carry out the plan.

Much of what we consider to be decision making is really problem solving. We see a problem, examine it, review various solutions, choose a solution, implement it, and follow up on it. This is a form of decision making but tends to be more like operational decision making. It tends to be curative in nature rather than preventative. It deals with a problem once it exists rather than with trying to prevent a problem from occurring in the first place.

Strategic decision making is preventative in nature. It is integral to the planning process in that, like planning, it is anticipatory in nature. Just as plans deal with the future, so do strategic decisions. The focus is on making major decisions that commit the organization to a direction for some time during the future. These direction-setting decisions usually involve a commitment of resources to a course of action at the exclusion of alternative courses of action.

Planning and strategic decision making are fundamental activities in any organization and should never be taken lightly. Because of this importance, many managers (even those at the top) sometimes shun this activity. They are afraid that they will make a mistake. However, simply avoiding this activity does not make it go away. Planning and decision making will still get done but it will be done by other people who probably should not be doing it, and it will be done on an ad hoc rather than a carefully thought out, integrated basis.

Therefore, a key element for effective strategic planning is a willingness to make the strategic decisions necessary in the planning process. Without this willingness, planning simply becomes a paper exercise. We can play school and write a nice plan but the decisions necessary to implement it are never made.

IS STRATEGIC PLANNING REALLY THAT NECESSARY?

This question usually implies this: Is strategic planning necessary for successful performance? The answer is, not necessarily. We all can think of people and firms that are successful that do not appear to have a strategic plan. At least they do not have a strategic plan as we discuss it in this book—a written, comprehensive, long-range plan that gives overall direction to the organization: a plan that is formalized.

Yet even in these organizations, top managers usually have a vision of where they would like to take the company. It may only be a mental vision, but it is, nevertheless, a vision. They clearly see where they want to go and how they wish to get there. This vision serves as an overall road map or plan of operation.

Therefore, the issue becomes, is it necessary to have a formalized plan—one that is written, comprehensive, and formally adopted by the organization?

Communication. In most organizations today, even smaller organizations, it is necessary to have such a plan. The advantage of a written plan that has been formally adopted by top management is that it is more easily communicated to those who must live with it. It also serves as an anchor or benchmark for action. It is not always easy to see someone else's vision on the direction of the company. In small companies where people are located in close proximity and have a great deal of face-to-face interaction, it certainly is easier to have a shared vision.

But as companies grow or where operations are geographically dispersed, the opportunity for a great deal of face-to-face interaction is reduced. Hence, communication becomes more difficult. Putting something in writing—formalizing the plan—becomes a necessary communication device. Since most companies wish to grow, even smaller companies soon see the necessity of having a formalized written plan.

But there is another advantage to having a formalized plan. The process of formalizing a plan causes a manager to share his vision of the future with others. The process of sharing, explaining, and defending a plan during a formal planning session sharpens the plan. It becomes clearer what the implicit vision really is. In addition, the discussion of the plan allows for two-way communication. The people with the vision may modify it based on comments and suggestions received.

Decision Making. A written plan serves another purpose: it is a permanent record and, therefore, can be used as a guideline or benchmark for important decisions that arise during the planning period. For example, a good strategic plan can provide answers for these important organizational decisions:

1. What type of personnel should we hire?
2. Do we need to expand our offices or plant?
3. Should we pay a higher wage? If so, how much higher?
4. Do we need to automate more?
5. Are we growing "enough"?
6. What is our profit level compared to our competitors?

7. Should we add a new product or service line?
8. Are some of our products/services obsolete?
9. Should we make acquisitions or divestitures?

These are but some of the key decisions a plan can provide guidance on. Every time we make a decision, we need to ask: how does this fit into our strategic plan? For example, if our plan calls for an increased marketing effort with heavier levels of promotion, a decision to add staff to the marketing department (i.e., how many people and their desired qualifications) will be based on the plan. If the plan calls for doubling the marketing effort with heavier emphasis on consumer merchandising, we will need to increase our marketing staff by a certain number of people (perhaps 50 percent), and we will need to ensure that they have consumer merchandising skills. In the absence of a formalized plan, the decision to hire is usually made on the basis of personal whim or the pressing contingencies of the moment, not on the basis of what is in the best long-term interests of the organization.

Orientation. A good plan also serves to orient new members to the organization. People come and go. We don't want the overall direction of the organization coming and going with them. We need stability regardless of who is in positions of power. A plan can give this stability. When we recruit prospective employees, we can show them our plan and discuss it with them to see if they believe they will fit in with the direction of the company. When we hire new employees, we can use the plan as an orientation tool so they know how their job fits into the total scheme of things. They will see that they are a member of an important team. This is very important to develop cooperation, coordination, and unity of effort. People need to be able to see how the whole picture fits together.

We can design our specific orientation and training programs around specific aspects of our plan. For example, for the new marketing people we hire in consumer merchandising, we would provide orientation and training on the merchandising skills and techniques we would like them to use to sell our product. We would tie these into specific sales goals we have set and to specific budget constraints they need to work within. Our training and orientation programs are anchored to the plan.

Evaluation. A formalized written plan makes it much easier to perform evaluations during and at the end of the planning period. The subjectivity is reduced. We look at what we said we would do and we make a judgment as to how well we actually did it. Since the plan is clearly spelled out in writing, the amount of disagreement over what we said we would do is substantially reduced. (It is never eliminated.)

For example, if we said in our plan we wanted to increase sales by a certain amount and reduce sales costs by a certain percentage, we could measure whether we had done this at the end of the planning period. Instead, if we had simply said "sell more," without formalizing it in a plan, we could sell more but actually lose money. Our expenses could go up faster than our sales. (Marginal costs exceed marginal revenues.) Of course, we would not want this. A good, written strategic plan should make it perfectly clear what is desired. If it does not, then it needs to be re-worked until it is clear.

BUT WE HAVE MBO, DO WE ALSO NEED A STRATEGIC PLAN?

Unless the organization has a top-to-bottom comprehensive MBO system, it usually needs a strategic plan. MBO is usually just the operational aspects of the strategic plan. It usually does not deal with the strategic aspects. That is, it usually does not include the environmental analysis and forecast and competitor and market analysis found in the strategic plan. MBO is more inward directed while strategic planning is more outward directed. Strategic planning attempts to place the organization in its environmental niche. It explains where and how the organization fits into the scheme of things: where it is and where it is going.

However, an organization using MBO is well on its way to strategic planning. It usually can expand MBO at the front end to do some environmental analysis and forecasting as well as competitor and market analysis. In fact, they will find that their objectives tend to be better ones when anchored against a more comprehensive strategic plan.

IS IT REALLY WORTHWHILE TO DO ALL THIS PLANNING WHEN WE LIVE IN A JUNGLE?

This question usually implies that the organization lives in such a turbulent environment that it is just about impossible to plan. In other words, just about the time we determine our environmental niche and where we want to go, the whole ball game changes. A new technology is developed. A new competitor enters the market, such as IBM entering the personal computer market. A new law is passed that significantly affects operations, such as the Occupational Safety and Health Act of 1970 (OSHA). An energy crisis develops. The list seems endless. Our carefully laid out plan is blown out of the water.

The ironic part about all this is that, when an organization lives in such an environment, it needs planning the most. The time when it is the hardest to plan is also the time when it is most needed. If every year is like the previous year, then why plan? We can just keep doing what we have been doing if we've been successful.

Fortunately, there are some methods that can be used to deal with environmental uncertainty. Later on in this book, we discuss environmental forecasting, scenario building, and contingency planning—all very useful techniques that can be used to deal with an uncertain environment. These techniques do not eliminate environmental uncertainty but they do give us some good tools to deal with it. We should not throw up our hands in a state of frustration, refusing to plan ever again because something happened that necessitates a major re-focusing of our plan. All plans need to be flexible as we shall see later in the book.

2.

How Should Strategic Planning Be Carried Out?

Many companies have participated in strategic planning only to see their efforts fail. One reason strategic planning fails is because the actual planning process was poorly structured and implemented. Unfortunately, in these companies strategic planning has a bad name even though it was the process used that should be faulted. Therefore, it is very important to the success of the process that it be properly implemented. This is not to imply that there is only one way to implement the process: actually there are several ways. However, this chapter focuses on a procedure I have used successfully with a wide variety of business and governmental organizations.

WHO SHOULD BE INVOLVED WITH STRATEGIC PLANNING?

Strategic planning must start at the top of the organization. In an organization with rather autonomous units, it can start at the top of any unit even though it may not be done at the very top of the organization. However, since the decisions involved in strategic planning are so fundamental and set the direction for the organization, top management, often including the board of directors or a board committee, should be involved at some point.

Beyond top management, the planning process will involve a number of different groups. In general, the process should be kept as participative as possible, given the time constraints present. People are usually more committed to a strategic plan if they have had some input in designing it.

Lower-Level Managers. These individuals should not be involved in actually writing the plan but certainly should have some input in formulating it. For example, we might ask sales managers for ideas on new product development strategies. We might also ask production managers for ideas on cost containment or quality improvement. We might ask supervisors for ideas on increasing employee involvement in decision making. These people are usually a rich, but often underutilized, information resource and should be used more often.

Staff Managers. Because of the vast quantity of information needed to generate most strategic plans, there usually is a need for staff assistance. These individuals are usually charged with helping to gather, analyze, and report information important for constructing the plan. The danger here is turning over the entire planning process to these people. Sometimes line managers abdicate their responsibility in planning because they think that their staff will take care of it. This is a critical mistake. Strategic planning is the responsibility of management—particularly top management. Staff only exists in a supportive, advisory position to help managers do better planning.

The cover story of the September 13, 1984 issue of *Business Week* pointed out the failure of relying on number-crunching professional staff people as the primary corporate planners. The article argues for much more involvement of line managers. Pages 64–65 of the article present an analysis of plans that failed and ones that worked.

The article analyzes 33 strategies described in various *Business Week* issues during 1979 and 1980. Nineteen were deemed to be in trouble or to have failed. Fourteen were evaluated as being successful. Some of the companies deemed to have unsuccessful plans were Ashland Oil, Campbell Soup, Exxon, and Lone Star Industries. The reasons for a failed plan involved such factors as poor acquisitions, misreading the market, management timidity, improper timing, increases in resource costs, and a failure to deal with deregulation.

Some of the companies with a plan deemed to have succeeded were Abbott Laboratories, American Motors, Bekins, Ralston Purina, and Uniroyal. Reasons for successful plans included modernizing equipment, increasing market share, introducing new products, diversifying products and resource base, and shedding many losing acquisitions.

While we might argue with the specific judgments made in the article as to which firms had successful plans and which ones had unsuccessful ones, the underlying theme of the evaluation is that successful plans were developed in companies that actively involved their line managers in the planning process. Planning was not done by "someone over in planning" but was seen as an integral part of the management process.

This makes sense. After all, the line manager knows more about the operations than the staff manager. And in the final analysis, the success of any strategic plan rests on the ability of the line managers to accomplish it. Thus, implementation is the key. There is a role for staff to play and there is a role for line management to play. Staff can collect, analyze, summarize, and submit data to line management. They can even offer suggestions on specific strategies and courses of action. But it is line management who should finally write the plan.

Of course, the old nemesis of line-staff conflict can rear its head here. There are many reasons for this conflict, but primary among them is the fact that even though staff people are usually experts in a specialized area and have access to so much information, they have no direct line authority. They may often have an advanced degree such as an MBA. They may actually know more about a particular topic than line managers and, consequently, want to tell line managers what to do. If the line manager does not follow the "advice," the staff manager becomes agitated and wonders why the line manager does not see the light.

THEN WHAT IS THE BEST WAY TO WORK WITH STAFF TO MINIMIZE CONFLICT?

The thesis of this manual is that strategic planning can and must be done by line managers. But in most organizations, line managers are very busy. They have production and sales deadlines to meet. They must live within tight budget guidelines. They are concerned with many aspects of the total operations—people, processes, machines, markets, regulations, and so on. They need staff to help. Sometimes, in smaller organizations there is no staff management present. In these instances, the line manager must either do all the analysis and planning or use an outside consultant to help with the process. If an outside consultant is used, he or she should be used in a staff capacity. Just as staff should not have sole responsibility for developing the plan, neither should an outside consultant. So the issue becomes how can we best work with staff or consultants to develop a plan. Here are some guidelines:

- Select your staff or consultant carefully. They should have some knowledge of both your business and of analytical and planning skills. They should be easy to work with and recognize that they will work in a support capacity. You are in charge.
- Define the scope of planning authority the staff or consultant is to have. The specific authority should be determined as follows: whom does the staff person report to; which specific people report to the staff person; and what specific activities will the staff person be responsible for.
- Determine the means that will be used to evaluate the performance of the staff, including the basis for any rewards such as merit salary increases. What, specifically, is the expected performance of the staff or consultants? Expectations and the rewards (e.g., salary increases, promotions, etc.) should be clearly stated at the onset.

In all of the above it is important to determine the overall relationship you want with staff. There should be mutual agreement on this relationship. There are at least four possible relationships that can exist.

Arm's Length. Here the staff or committee simply gathers data and provides it to line management without any analysis. This is seldom used, but if line management has the time and inclination to wade through data or if the data are not very extensive, it can be a fruitful relationship.

Friendly Acquaintance. Here the staff not only gathers the data but also analyzes it. Tables, graphs, figures, and summaries are developed. However, no recommendations are provided. This is more common than the first case.

Good Friend. Here the staff gathers the data, analyzes them, and develops several alternative courses of action without recommending a specific course. Line managers make the final choice. This is a very common arrangement.

Let's Get Married. Here the staff does all the above but goes one step further. A specific recommendation is made and justified. The staff or consultant may even have some authority to begin implementation. This also is very common but may become less so in view of the thinking today that staff are actually too much involved with writing the plan.

In some instances, the company may actually follow a principle called *compulsory staff advice.* In this case no management action can be taken without first running it by staff for their review. If we decide, for example, to build a new plant, we may first have to receive a suggestion from staff as to where it should be located before we decide where to build it. We don't actually have to follow the staff advice, but we do have to receive it.

Therefore, when specifying the authority, duties, and expectations, it is important that top management determine the type of relationship desired between line and staff at the onset. This will serve as the basis for specific working relationships.

BUT WHAT IF THINGS DON'T WORK OUT AND CONFLICT WITH STAFF OCCURS?

From time to time conflict between line and staff will occur. Sometimes it dies out of its own accord. Sometimes the two parties can work it out through negotiation and compromise. But in the final analysis line management must resolve the conflict since they are the ones ultimately responsible and accountable for performance. This means top management may need to get involved either in the role of a mediator or as an arbitrator if the conflict occurs between mid-level line managers and staff.

If conflict occurs on a regular or frequent basis, then the basic relationship and duties between line and staff should be examined. There are probably some ill-defined duties or other misunderstandings that need to be clarified. Occasionally, the conflict can be caused by an arrogant personality of one of the parties. This may require that the individual be removed from the planning team.

HOW CAN COMMITTEES BE BEST USED IN THE PLANNING PROCESS?

Almost all organizations committed to strategic planning use a committee and subcommittees to facilitate the process. The main committee is usually made up of some board members, top-level executives, a few key staff people, and often one or two operating managers. It is a good idea to keep the size of the committee between 10 and 20 people.

The essential elements for a successful committee are as follows:

• Pick those who have an interest and expertise in strategic planning.
• Be sure the committee has a charge that is clearly understood and a date for task accomplishment.
• Be sure the committee has the full confidence of top management and is simply not a sham.
• Be sure the committee has both the authority to request information and to recommend action based on it.

The committee usually acts in an advisory capacity to top management. They often include some staff people and they use data generated by staff. They usually prepare a draft of the entire plan or specific portions of it for review and action by top management during planning meetings. Seldom does the committee actually adopt the plan for the entire organization; rather, it is better to leave final adoption up to top management.

The Role of Commitment. Making the final say on the plan a key responsibility of top management rather than a committee or staff group is very important for final plan implementation. So often an organization will spend much time and money developing a strategic plan only to fail in implementation. The plan becomes a nice document that sits on peoples' shelves and is seldom if ever consulted. One reason for this failure is because top management never really becomes fully committed to the planning process. Rather, it is viewed as something being done by "that committee" or by "those staff people." People throughout the organization must view the plan as having full and complete commitment from top management if the plan is to have credibility throughout the organization.

HOW SHOULD WORKSHOPS BE USED IN PLANNING?

Very often the focus of the strategic planning process is a series of workshops. It is in these workshops that the plan is developed and discussed. In some cases it may be adopted during a workshop. The workshops are usually made up of members of the planning committee or an executive committee plus a few others as needed. Once again, caution should be exercised here so that too large a group does not become directly involved in the workshop or the workshop will become unwieldy. Frequently, workshop sessions can be held with subcommittees of the planning committee.

The Use of a Group Facilitator. It is often helpful to use a group facilitator to manage the discussion in the workshop. This person can be either someone from outside the organization who consults in the area of strategic planning or someone within the organization. If someone from within the organization is chosen, it is important that it be a person who is well respected and who is knowledgeable about both strategic planning and group processes. The person should also be viewed as objective. It is not a good idea to have the CEO or other high authority figure run the workshops since this may stifle free and open discussion.

Format for Workshops. There are three phases for each workshop: (1) preparation and data gathering, (2) group discussion, and (3) follow-up and evaluation. To get the most out of the workshop, the participants should come prepared. This means that they need to be familiar with strategic planning, if they are not already, and that they need to study any information to be discussed at the workshop. They also need to feel free to participate fully during the workshop discussion without fear of recrimination.

There are basically three types of strategic planning workshops that are helpful. They may be done alone or in conjunction with each other. Of course, there are variations of each depending on the needs of the particular organization.

The Short Overview. The short overview consists of a three-hour lecture-discussion of strategic planning and decision making. (This could be expanded to six hours if desired.) The entire process is broadly reviewed and the various steps and forms that can be used are explained.

This type of workshop can handle a fairly large number of people. Board members and top- and perhaps some middle-level managers would find this enlightening. Even for a company well into a formalized strategic planning process, the workshop is useful as a check whereby executives can compare what they do with an alternative comprehensive process. Since there are many versions of strategic planning in use, a company may wish to compare what it does to a different version of the process.

Of course, if a firm is doing little or no formalized strategic planning, this workshop presents a suggested approach for their consideration. It allows them to test the waters and to experiment to determine whether they want to undertake a formalized strategic planning process.

Essentially, the three-to-six-hour workshop could cover these points:

• strategic planning—what it is and is not
• strategic decision making
• role of boards, executives, and staff
• environmental analysis and forecasting
• market/customer analysis
• internal assessment
• mission analysis
• making planning assumptions
• developing strategic thrusts
• formulating goals and objectives
• developing action steps to reach objectives
• budgeting and control
• evaluation and adjustment

Of course, in three hours, each point above is only briefly discussed.

The Planning Retreat. A very common strategic planning workshop is a retreat. Essentially, this is a 12-to-15-hour workshop (away from the office) that involves the planning or executive committee in writing or revising the strategic plan. (In order to have full participation, the workshop should be limited to 10 to 15 active participants. Others might be present, but active participation should be limited.)

The workshop can be used with an organization that now has a plan and wishes to evaluate and revise it. It also can be used with one that is beginning its first effort in formalized strategic planning. A suggested agenda for the workshop is as follows:

• overview of strategic planning and decision making (2 hours)
• board, management, and staff roles (1 hour)
• worksheet preparation for each step in the process (6 hours)
• tie-in worksheets (2 hours)
• implementing the plan—getting commitments and making it work (1 hour)

The hours for the planning retreat can be adjusted depending on the specific needs of the group down to 9 hours or up to 18 hours.

It is best to conduct the workshop in a retreat-like atmosphere away from the office, but this is not absolutely necessary. A conference facility at a local hotel or a resort in the mountains or at the beach both work well. If a resort is used, spouses can be invited to help enhance the after-hours social and recreational opportunities for the participants. (Some may disagree with just how much enhancement actually occurs.) The sessions can be held over three or four half days if desired so recreation and leisure time is available. Perhaps it could even be tied to a weekend.

The workshops are usually quite intensive. A consultant may act as a moderator, facilitator, and recorder. The group actually writes the plan, not the consultant. Usually, there is much open discussion and give and take. Occasionally, there are arguments. One advantage of using an outside facilitator is to smooth over the arguments. The facilitator can also keep the discussion on track and prohibit certain individuals from dominating the discussion. He or she can also draw out those who may be reluctant to speak up.

Prior to the workshop, the participants should review the following items:

- any forecasts that have been prepared, such as an economic forecast
- this year's and last year's budgets (Next year's budget should be developed either at the workshop or after it.)
- last year's and this year's goals (if they exist)
- employee turnover, absence, tardiness, grievance, and productivity rates
- any market or industry surveys
- articles and strategic planning forms that are to be used
- annual company reports
- competitor actions

Good preliminary work will make the workshop much more productive.

The Phased Workshop. The last strategic planning and decision-making format is more comprehensive than the first two versions. Under this version, at least three meetings are held. The first meeting, which usually lasts about a day, reviews the strategic planning and decision-making process in some depth, and an effort is made to examine the past, present, and/or potential success the organization is likely to have with the process.

Next, a four-to-six-week data gathering period occurs where the company gathers data about its performance. At least the items listed above should be examined, but the organization may wish to go beyond this list and also include such items as data-processing procedures, equipment and machinery use, office layout, paperwork and communication flow, and other operations factors. This operations analysis is very helpful for good planning.

Following this, the retreat-like planning and decision-making workshop as described above is held.

The last step involves a final one-day meeting (which may be repeated periodically) at least three months after the adoption of the plan. At this workshop, an evaluation of the plan is made. Roadblocks as well as successes are noted. Adjustments and refinements are suggested. This may be repeated as many as four times before a new plan for the coming planning period is developed.

WHAT ARE SOME PROBLEMS TO WATCH OUT FOR IN CONDUCTING THE WORKSHOPS?

Hidden Agendas. Very often, participants will bring a hidden agenda with them to the workshop. It is important to expose these agendas if they begin to interfere with the planning process. The group facilitator is charged with this responsibility. These agendas could include any of the following topics: a desire to subvert the planning process for whatever reason; a pet project that a participant or group of participants are pushing; viewing the retreat more as a social and recreational function rather than a work one; the opportunity to carry through with a personal vendetta; or, on rare occasions, the opportunity to exercise a major power play. Any one of these issues can subvert the workshop and, therefore, must be dealt with directly.

There are several ways to recognize and deal with hidden agendas as follows:

Prevent It. If the group facilitator does a good job in setting the proper climate for the workshop at the onset, he or she may prevent the hidden agenda from becoming a problem. This can be done by telling the participants that the workshop will encourage free and open communication among participants without fear of retribution.

Ignore It. Bring discussion back on target hoping that those who raise tangential points will soon cease.

Expose It. Let the individuals have their say and question them about the issue. Bring it out on the table for all to see and discuss. If the hidden agenda won't go away, then it could be dealt with this way.

Call a Recess or Break. If it becomes apparent that a major hidden agenda is present and the participants will not lay it out on the table, the facilitator should call a break and talk with the participants who have the agenda to find out what is going on. A means to deal with the agenda should be developed during the break with those involved.

Schedule a Special Meeting to Deal with It. If the hidden agenda is a major issue that is serving to impede the planning workshop but the participants are unwilling to deal with it, it may be necessary to set up a special meeting just to deal with the item. This may be done during an afternoon at the workshop or may be done later after the workshop is concluded. If the hidden agenda is critical and not amenable to discussion at the time of the workshop, it may be necessary to recess the workshop for several weeks until the issue can be resolved.

Of course, none of the methods may work. The group may be playing games with the facilitator. If this happens, it is apparent that the group is not seriously interested in strategic planning and the facilitator should end the workshop. The group must have a certain amount of "planning readiness"—a real desire to plan—for any workshop to have the desired effect. A group facilitator usually cannot instill this desire for planning readiness but must come from decision makers in the group.

Unrealistic Expectations. Another problem that sometimes hinders the effectiveness of the planning workshop are inflated expectations. The planning group believes that all of the problems the firm has been experiencing over the years will be solved over the weekend. This is totally unrealistic. The workshop will set the stage for good problem solving and may even solve some of the problems, but it is unlikely that all the problems will be solved. As the workshop progresses, participants may become disenchanted as they see that all of the problems are not disappearing

The facilitator must make it clear at the outset that, while important problems will be examined during the workshop, they likely will not be solved. It should be stressed, however, that the strategic planning workshop will provide a framework for solving the problems that the participants can use as time passes.

Can't Commit to the Plan. Very often some people in the workshop will state that they cannot actually commit to the plan that is developed until more study is done. Even with extensive preliminary work, it may become apparent that more data and analysis is needed before a project or objective is firmed up. At this point, it should be made clear that the plan is flexible and amenable to change in light of additional data and analysis. No absolute commitments should be asked for. If it becomes apparent that major chunks of data and analysis are missing, then either a recess of several weeks should be called so the data can be obtained or the item can be temporarily passed up and returned to if the data can be obtained in a few hours.

Individual Dominance. Sometimes one or two key people will simply dominate all discussion. These people may be of high rank or may be people with long-time tenure with the organization. The group facilitator should not allow this to happen. Other people should be specifically called on by name for their views. The facilitator should announce, "Let's see what others have to say on the topic," as need be. If necessary, the facilitator should talk with those who dominate discussion during a break to tell them to hold it down.

Missing People. Sometimes an important member of the planning group will be unable to attend the workshop. The group must decide if it can go on without the person. Perhaps a substitute can be sent or someone else in the group can take the role of the missing person. The absence of one or two people should not keep the group from holding a planning workshop. It is difficult to get everyone together at any one time, so the workshop will likely be postponed indefinitely if we keep waiting for a convenient time for Fred.

Left Hanging. At the conclusion of the workshop, the facilitator should help the group summarize the next steps needed in the planning process. Specific steps, dates, and individual accountability should be specified. For example, we might say: "Cathie is to get the revised product cost figures to Jack by October 1 so modifications can be made in our second strategic thrust." Or "Henry is to reanalyze competitor market share and give it to Sally by October 20." People need to know what the next steps are in the planning process.

At a bare minimum it should be specified by what date the notes—i.e., sketch of the plan from the workshop—will be typed up and distributed to everyone for review. A date for a review meeting should be set. People need to feel a sense of closure.

HOW CAN THE PLANNING HORIZON BE DETERMINED?

Very frequently, a five-year planning horizon is selected for the strategic plan. Within the overall plan are one-year operational plans. This time format can vary depending on the nature of the organizational operations and product/service line. For example, a company that faces a three-year operating cycle based on economic conditions, such as a commercial construction company, may wish to be on a three-year strategic plan. A governmental agency that faces biennial budgeting may wish to be on a two-year strategic plan. A company in a rapidly changing environment, such as personal computers, may wish to be on a two- or three-year plan.

Regardless of the planning period selected, the annual review usually involves lopping off the past year and adding the next coming year beyond the existing plan. Thus, if our plan goes through 1991, at the end of 1987, we would drop that year and add 1992 if our planning horizon were five years.

Some companies actually try to plan beyond five years. For example, General Electric has pioneered long-range planning and has developed a section concerned primarily with futurism. Their task is to look far into the future and to identify trends that may occur 20 years from now so that GE can begin to do product research and development today on products that will meet people's needs many years from now. With the long lead time to develop many of today's products, this is a good idea. Of course, there is always the possibility that a major change in technology in a related or unrelated field may obviate the need for the product.

Companies that do plan far into the future often develop specific short-, intermediate-, and long-term plans that integrate with each other. Short-term plans are usually defined as one year or less in time, intermediate as two to four years, and long-term as five years or more in length. The important point is to make sure that all three plans do tie in with one another.

HOW CAN CONFLICTS IN THE PLANNING PROCESS BE RESOLVED?

If the planning participants really take the planning process seriously, there are likely to be many points of disagreement along the way. These may occur during the workshop, as discussed above, or may occur at other times outside of the workshops. It is important to resolve these arguments as best as possible. Since we are discussing fundamental questions about the future of the company in an uncertain environment, there may be a substantial amount of disagreement. There are some things that can be done to resolve these conflicts.

- Make sure the necessary data and other information are available for all involved. There should be minimum disagreement over historical facts.
- Be sure that facts are clearly distinguished from opinions and assumptions during any discussion, presentation, or report.
- Let people have their say but don't let an individual dominate the discussion at any point in the planning process. Let people have the opportunity to get things off their chest but not hog the show.
- Avoid shouting matches. If things begin to get out of hand, call for a recess, even if it is just an office discussion.
- Use social time to bring warring factions together over a drink, meal, game of golf, or at a party.
- During extended periods of debate, remind people of the need to bring closure to the planning process by the previously agreed upon date.

The use of a group facilitator who is skilled in group processes can aid substantially in managing the conflict that is likely to occur during the workshop discussions as we discussed. Outside of the workshop, the company planning coordinator needs to take the initiative.

HOW CAN PLANS BE IMPLEMENTED?

As has been indicated previously, there are many factors that can hinder the effective implementation of strategic planning. These factors need to be explicitly recognized at the outset if the planning process is to lead to final implementation. Let's look at these planning barriers.

- *No time to plan.* Participants are so caught up in their daily routine that they believe they do not have any time to do planning. They are spending too much post hoc time and not enough front-end time.
- *Too many crises and changing priorities.* Here people feel that there is no sense in planning since priorities change so quickly that the plan soon becomes meaningless. Usually this is caused by a lack of proper forecasting.
- *Information overload.* Since strategic planning requires a great deal of information, people feel overwhelmed. Keep information down to what is absolutely necessary and use the computer to help manage it.
- *Too much paperwork.* This is closely related to the above. People feel that all they do on their job is to fill out strategic planning forms. Keep these forms to an absolute minimum and use the computer to store and report planning information.
- *Too much politics.* "Planning is a rational and logical process and our operation is just too political for it to work." This complaint is common in government organizations, but one also hears it in some large companies. Recognize the politics, don't ignore them, and build them into the planning process. Let people have their say.
- *Don't play school.* Use the plan. Refer to it in staff meetings. Look at it when decisions are to be made. Tie it into the management performance appraisal process and to evaluation and control. This issue is discussed later in this manual.

There are other reasons why planning may fail, but these are the more common ones. It is a good idea to address these specifically at some point during the workshop sessions and other meetings and ask the group what can be done to prevent, reduce, or eliminate them. One last thought here: no plan will ever get implemented unless the question of "who is going to do what and when" is specifically answered. The planning process presented in this manual forces participants to address this question specifically as part of the process.

3.

Environmental Analysis: Status Quo

We are now ready to begin the actual strategic planning process. The first step in the process is to look outside the organization at the environment that affects it. This action is one key factor that distinguishes strategic planning from regular planning. We do this because we know that there are many outside forces that have a major effect on our internal operations. We are particularly interested in identifying environmental opportunities and constraints faced by our organization. We do not want to plan in a vacuum.

WHAT IS ENVIRONMENTAL SCANNING?

Environmental scanning involves a comprehensive and systematic examination of significant aspects of the outside environment. A judgment is made as to how these aspects affect the organization. Environmental scanning should be a continuous process. Even though every manager is partially responsible for this activity, in large companies, such as GE, a staff group may help. This scan is summarized periodically for the planning workshops and meetings.

HOW IS ENVIRONMENTAL SCANNING USED?

For environmental scanning to be useful, it must be integrated into the planning process. This means that the participants must be willing to look outward before they look inward. Sometimes it is difficult to change this inward orientation since the day-to-day job of line managers fosters a here-and-now job orientation.

One way to break this orientation is initially to present key information about the environment in almost a startling fashion without all the statistics. Once the attention of the line manager is gotten, the statistical information can be added later. For example, among a group of bankers, the initial discussion of the environment might begin by making a case why Sears is the major competitor in personal banking. (For example, see Steve Weiner and Frank Jones, "Sears, A Power in Many Fields Now, Looks Into New Ones: Financial Services Businesses Appear Certain to Grow," *Wall Street Journal,* February 10, 1984, p. 10.) While this probably overstates the case, it would lead to a discussion of how the environment for banking services is changing. This could be followed up with a discussion of the activities of not only Sears, but also savings and loans, credit unions, and other institutions in traditional banking activities. A discussion of legal, political, and economic factors that made this possible would then be held.

HOW DO WE TELL WHICH ASPECTS OF THE ENVIRONMENT ARE RELEVANT?

For many managers, the outside environment is difficult to conceptualize for planning purposes. They see a large abstract mass of unstructured information about which they may feel they know little about. Thus, one of the first steps involved in environmental analysis is environmental scoping. This involves narrowing down the outside environment to areas that are relevant to the organization. This is a key activity to help prevent information overload.

As shown in Exhibit 2, we can divide the outside environment into three main sectors: the relevant environment, the potentially relevant environment, and the non-relevant environment. We can use these ideas to establish a domain for the organization. And if we can get agreement among various important groups that affect our organization, we can achieve domain consensus. Let's briefly examine each of these ideas in more detail.

Relevant Environment. This is the aspect of the outside environment that is of immediate relevance for goal setting. This environment consists of factors that we must consider when we set our goals. Usually included in this environment are suppliers, distributors, competitors, the local labor market, lenders, owners, unions, and pertinent laws. For example, for a manufacturer of fiberglass surfboards, this environment would consist of suppliers of resin and fiberglass, the distribution network, availability of local labor, other manufacturers of surfboards, stockholders, OSHA requirements on safety (plus other laws), and lenders. We are not really concerned with the customer or market at this point, although we do examine it at a later stage of the process. Nor are we concerned with the overall general economy here, although we should be concerned with economic conditions in our particular industry. Finally, we are not concerned at this point with forecasting these factors, although we do add forecasting later.

Exhibit 2
Scoping the Outside Environment

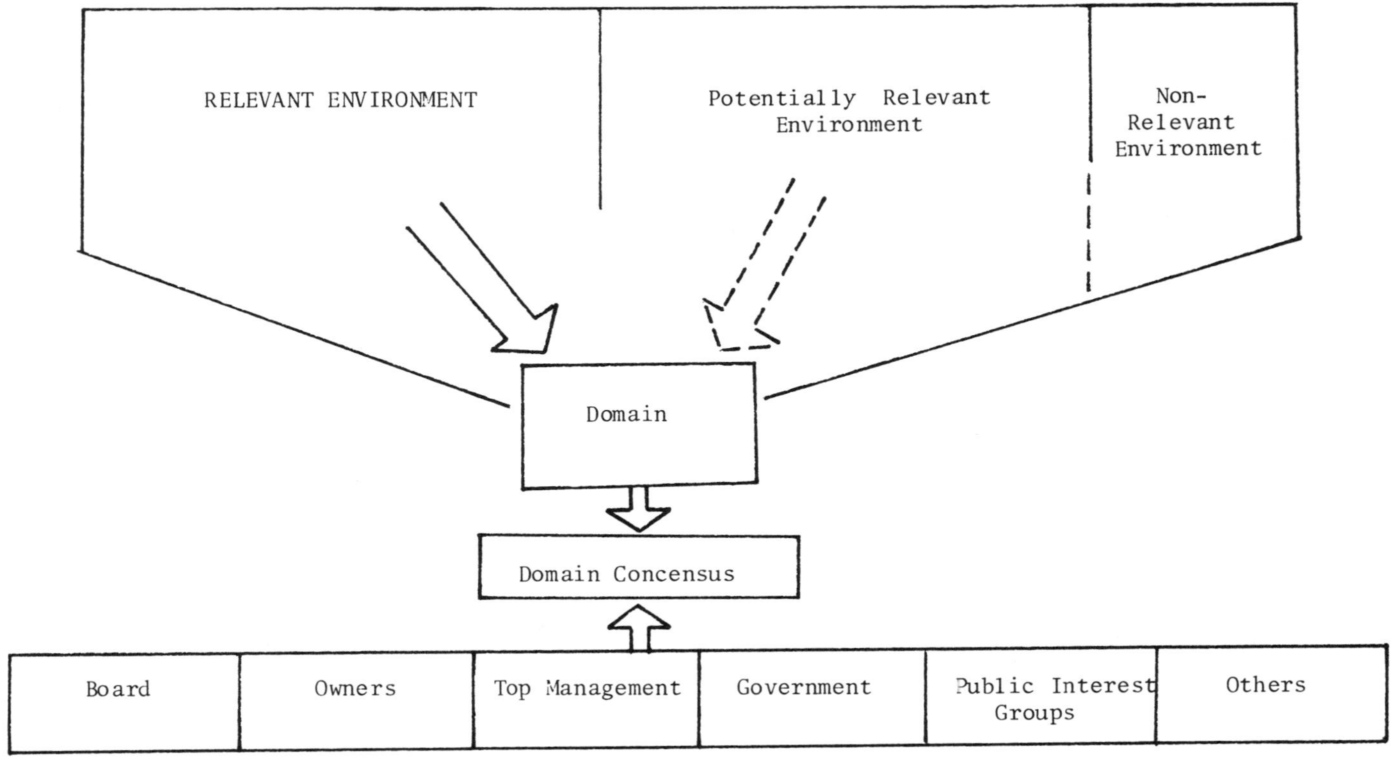

Potentially Relevant Environment. This is the outside environment that is potentially relevant to goal setting. It consists of those factors on the periphery of our immediate environment. For example, depending on our company and industry, this environment could consist of international conditions, secondary competitors, secondary suppliers, and alternative distribution networks. We cannot ignore this environment because sometimes aspects of this environment can move into the relevant environment. But we do not need to spend as much time and effort scanning our potentially relevant environment as we do our relevant environment. We must be cautious here: for example, many companies were badly hurt during the Arab oil crisis of the seventies when their primary oil supply dried up. Those that had alternative sources of supply or could burn coal instead of oil fared much better. Therefore, we must be aware of possible situations that could cause a part of our potential environment suddenly to become part of our immediate environment.

Non-relevant Environment. This is the part of our outside environment that we can pretty safely ignore. We cannot completely ignore it, but we need only be casually interested in it. For example, General Motors does not need to monitor the price of soybeans as part of their planning process. Our surfboard manufacturer need not be concerned with the price of Cadillacs. However, if GM began to use substantially more fiberglass in automobiles, the surfboard manufacturer would be interested in this because of what might happen to the price of fiberglass and resin.

Domain. We can use the above ideas to determine the domain for our organization. The domain is the specific part of the outside environment we stake out for ourselves. It is as if we put a fence around part of our outside environment and then formally announce to everyone that this is what really matters to us.

The domain consists of the market(s) we intend to serve, the products and services we intend to provide to this market, and the geographic location of the market. Usually, when we discuss our domain we also discuss our organizational mission. This is okay, but a detailed discussion and formulation of the mission statement should be postponed to a later step in the process. We really do not want to formulate our mission until we fully examine our market, environment, and internal strengths and weaknesses and prepare a forecast as to what the environment and market hold for us.

Domain Consensus. This occurs when everyone of importance agrees on the domain. We have general agreement among owners, top management, government agencies, etc., about what we should be doing and where we should be doing it. Some organizations never really reach a consensus. This makes it very difficult to plan since there is a great deal of disagreement about the nature of the business of the organization. Consequently, a concerted attempt should be made to try to find a workable, even if imperfect, consensus.

WHAT ARE KEY SEGMENTS OF THE ENVIRONMENT?

The importance of various parts of the environment will vary depending upon the nature of the organization's business. Regardless, the general components of the outside environment are similar. In this section, we review these components.

Economy. Every organization must be aware of the general state of economic conditions at the national, regional, and local level. Probably no other area of the outside environment so directly affects a firm's operations. Some of the data that should be tracked are interest rates, GNP, unemployment rates, leading indicators, and inflation. Also, prices of certain commodities may need to be closely watched. Information on the economy can be obtained by reading business periodicals, such as the *Wall Street Journal* and *Business Week;* by reading the various Federal Reserve Bulletins; and by subscribing to services of various economic forecasting firms, such as Chase Econometrics.

It is important to remember that at this stage of the strategic planning process we want only to assess the present state of economic activity. At a later stage we will want to forecast economic information.

Competition. Here we are concerned with specifically identifying our competition and how they affect us. We should identify both those firms that directly and indirectly compete with us. Our objective here is to look at their products, services, and strategies relative to our own. From this we can develop our competitive advantage, which is how we differ from our competition. It answers the question: Why would someone buy our product or service over our competitor's?

Legal/Political. The major laws and political climate as they affect us are examined here. These will include federal, state, local, and international law. Laws in employment, product safety, pollution control, safety and health, advertising, and contracts are some of the areas we would examine. Depending on our industry, other laws may be pertinent. For example, if we are in the banking industry, there would be a whole host of federal and state laws we would also need to examine. The main objective here is to ensure that we are in compliance with the legislation. Competent legal advice is essential here.

Social. Here we are concerned with identifying the major social values and norms that are affecting our operations. For example, we may see a trend toward more individual attention and convenience occurring in society. We would need to speculate as to how that is affecting our operations. Good sources for this information are magazines, trade journals, general business periodicals such as the *Wall Street Journal,* and consultants who specialize in social analysis.

Demographics. This area deals with statistical information about population. For example, mean age, income, and family size of people in an area are common demographic data. So are net migration figures, population growth, birth and death rates, travel rates, and employment figures. Other demographic data may be important depending on the firm's line of business. For example, an art museum might be interested in the average education level of the local population in planning art exhibits. The local chamber of commerce and the U.S. Census Bureau are good sources for this information. Census data are available at most any university library. Also, market research firms will do custom studies for local areas and industries. An excellent magazine in the field is called *American Demographics* from Dow Jones and Co. (Write *American Demographics*, P.O. Box 68, Ithaca, N.Y. 14581.)

Technology. The technology available for a particular process or operation should be carefully reviewed. Also, technologies in related fields should be reviewed to determine the applicability to our operations. The technology used by our competitors especially should be reviewed—this includes any overseas competition. The steel industry would have been well advised to review the technology employed by steel producers in Japan during the decade of the seventies in order to have avoided the technological obsolescence U.S. producers experienced in the early eighties. Trade journals and trade shows are excellent sources of information on this topic.

Labor Market. Both the local and national labor market should be reviewed. Unemployment rates, labor force participation rates, wage rates, skill distribution, educational level, and labor market growth are all important here. Data from the local chamber of commerce, U.S. Department of Labor, and the state office of business development are all good sources of information. Also, union hiring halls can be helpful in the skilled trades.

Key Physical Resources. If we are dependent on certain key physical resources, we should assess their availability. For example, if we produce photographic film, the availability of silver is of prime importance to us. If we produce catalytic converters for automobiles, the availability of platinum is important. We should thoroughly review our present and possible operations to assess the availability of key resources. Newsletters and commodity reports are good places to find this information.

Suppliers. We should thoroughly review our relationship with our suppliers. Past problems should be carefully analyzed. Competing suppliers should be reviewed for cost and service comparisons with those suppliers we are now using. Trade shows, trade magazines, brochures, and sales talks with suppliers are all good sources for this information.

Distributors. A similar review of our distributors should be held. In particular, we should review alternative distribution channels to see if they might be better options for distributing our products and services. Information on distribution channels can be obtained from similar sources as supplier information.

Transportation. Our transportation network should be reviewed. This is especially important today in view of the deregulation that has occurred in trucking and airlines. Rates and routes are under much more intense competition and cheaper, more efficient forms of transportation for our products might be available. Trade journals and transportation companies are good sources for information.

Energy Supplies. An assessment of key energy resources is critical for most firms today. Not only should the availability of present energy resources be reviewed, but also the availability of alternative resources. Energy suppliers as well as special publications on the topic, such as the *Lundberg Letter*, should be consulted.

International Conditions. Depending on the operation, international affairs might have a major bearing on our business. We should review the present political and economic state of other countries significant to our business, as well as the general level of international economic trade and monetary conditions. Special trade conferences and periodicals, such as the *Economist*, are helpful here.

HOW CAN ENVIRONMENTAL INFORMATION BE CLASSIFIED AS AN OPPORTUNITY OR A CONSTRAINT?

At this point, it is possible to feel overwhelmed by environmental information. This feeling will be lessened if we did a good job narrowing our environment to our relevant environment and our domain prior to the above scoping exercise. But we also need to do one other activity with this environmental information in order to get a handle on it: we need to categorize the information as to whether we see it as an opportunity or a constraint for us.

Environmental Opportunities. These are factors in the environment that provide new markets or advantages for us.

Environmental Constraints. These are threats in the environment that hinder the performance of our operations or keep us from reaching our objectives. What may be a threat or constraint for one firm might be an opportunity for another. For example, pollution control laws were viewed as a major constraint by most companies, especially coal-burning utilities. However, those companies in the pollution control business viewed these laws as a real opportunity. If we are in the business of selling smokestack scrubbers, we would welcome these environmental laws. Also, if we produced eastern U.S. hard coal, which is low in sulphur, we would welcome these laws more than if we produced high sulphur western coal. The following extract shows a summary of an

environmental scan for a large telecommunications company which reflects their view of environmental opportunities.

Geographically, we are the largest of the telecommunications companies in
our area. Yet geography is only one measure and certainly not the most im-
pressive measure of our strength.
We see high projections of our region's growth. Our marketing area is the
fastest developing in this country.
Personal income in our area is outpacing the rest of the country by 26 percent.
Our employment is lower, our average age is younger, and our housing starts per
capita are higher. The education of our people ranks at the top. The quality of
our work force is high and is valuable as a resource for growth. A recent study
compared wage, productivity, and education levels on a state-by-state basis. Our
region is home to 7 of the top 10 rated states in that study.
The traditional base of agriculture and forestry in our area is yielding its lead
to high technology and service-based industries, industries that require the kind
of telecommunications systems that we provide.
Our region abounds with natural resources that will promote the growth of
industry and enrich the life-styles of our residents, including 70 percent of the
known silica reserves in the 48 states, 90 percent of the nation's salt, 48 percent of
its gypsum, 51 percent of its coal, and 60 percent of its limestone. This area
provides 46 percent of the nation's supply of saw timber (critical to the recover-
ing housing market) and encompasses 57 percent of the national forest lands.
Forty percent of the nation's food product is rooted in our soil.
Five of the 10 cities of great opportunity, cited by John Naisbitt in his book,
Megatrends, are in our territory. Ours is a diverse and dynamic region, capable of
accommodating the evolving decentralization of America with land, natural resources, trained individuals, and a stimulating environment.
This environment is a natural setting for telecommunications growth. The
increasing base and the increasing capacity to service that base will nurture
continued progress.
We serve six of the fastest growing states in this country, populated by 27
million people. The new and developing industries of this country are increasingly dependent on the information their telecommunications system can
bring them.

In reviewing our environmental assessment, we want to categorize
factors we identify as either helping us to achieve our objectives and
facilitating our operation or hurting us in our operations. We also need
to be mindful of new opportunities our environment presents to us that
we are not now taking advantage of. We will revisit this analysis two more
times: when we make our environmental forecast and when we write our
strategic thrusts and objectives.
Exhibits 3 through 5 can help us to do this environmental analysis.
Exhibit 3 is a summary of key environmental factors and Exhibit 4 is a
workshop form for completing an environmental analysis. Exhibit 5 is
also presented for classifying factors into opportunities or constraints.

Exhibit 3
Environmental Assessment

Environmental Sector	Key Information	Information Sources
Economy	GNP, unemployment rates, leading indicators, inflation, commodity prices, interest rates	*Wall Street Journal, Business Week,* Federal Reserve Bulletins
Competition	Prices, products, services, technology, competitive edge	Trade shows, trade magazines, general business magazines, own customers
Legal/Political	State, federal, local legislation, administrative and court rulings	Newsletters, general business magazines, legal advice
Social	Values, norms, expectations	Trade journals, general business periodicals, consultants
Demographic	Age, sex, income, population growth, net migration, birth and death rates, family size, educational levels	U.S. Bureau of Census, local chambers of commerce, market research firms
Technology	Technological developments in competition and related areas, technological developments in data processing	Trade shows and trade journals, general business periodicals, EDP journals
Labor Market	Unemployment rates, wage rates, skill distribution, labor force participation rates, educational levels, labor force growth	U.S. Bureau of Labor Statistics, local chambers of commerce, state offices of business development, union hiring halls
Key Physical Resources	Commodities, minerals, precious metals, raw materials, semi-finished goods	Suppliers, market newsletters, commodity reports
Suppliers	Past practices and problems, pricing, service, competition	Delivery reports, alternative suppliers, trade shows and journals

Exhibit 3 (Continued)

Environmental Sector	Key Information	Information Sources
Distributors	Past practices and problems, service, information sending, collection, and payment	Sales and distribution reports, trade shows and journals, alternative distribution channels
Transportation	Rates, routes, speed, service, safety	Trade journals, transporters
Energy Supplies	Availability, delivery, price, alternatives, conservation factors	Energy suppliers, government reports, *Lundburg Letter*
International Conditions	International economy, economic trade, exchange rates, tariffs, political conditions	General business journals, trade conferences, *The Economist*

HOW CAN ENVIRONMENTAL INFORMATION BE GATHERED?

In the section above, we pointed out a number of areas in which to look for environmental information. But we also need to discuss the way environmental information enters the organization. The primary concept here is the idea of boundary spanning units. These are units within the organization whose job it is to link the organization to its environment. For example, a salesforce or employment recruiters are boundary spanning units.

Most organizations view these units as a one-way street—passing information from the organization to some sector of the environment. However, they should be viewed as having a dual function in that they should also gather information from the environment and bring it to the organization. For example, a salesforce should keep the firm informed on customer preferences, service needs, product problems, and so on so that this information can be used in designing new products and services. The same idea holds with employment recruiters. If they see that they are not able to attract the type of employee the firm desires, they should feel free to suggest changes in the employment package being offered. The point is, any unit that has environmental contact must try to communicate information about the environment to various management units in the organization that can do something about it.

In addition, there are people who are not in boundary spanning units in organizations who play a boundary spanning role. For example, the

Exhibit 4
Worksheet for Environmental Analysis

ENVIRONMENTAL SECTOR	KEY INFORMATION
Economy	
Competition	
Legal/Political	
Social	
Demographic	
Technology	
Labor Market	
Key Physical Resources	

Exhibit 4 (Continued)

ENVIRONMENTAL SECTOR	KEY INFORMATION
Suppliers	
Distributors	
Transportation	
Energy Supplies	
International Conditions	

Chief Executive Officer of a major corporation may spend more time on the road speaking before investor groups, colleges and universities, and Congressional committees than is spent at the home office. If the CEO keeps eyes and ears open, much valuable information about the environment can be gathered and used by the organization.

The same idea holds for others in the organization as they visit clients, attend trade shows and conferences, or otherwise interact with aspects of the outside environment. They have the responsibility to share information obtained with others in the organization when they return.

Finally, some organizations have specialized staffs whose job it is to obtain environmental information. These may be long-range planning staffs, such as GE's, or market research staffs. They may also buy environmental information from consultants or through subscriptions to newsletters. In most large organizations, a variety of methods are used to obtain this information.

HOW CAN THE ISSUES ANALYSIS METHOD BE USED TO EXAMINE THE ENVIRONMENT?

Several times we have mentioned the GE long-range planning staff. These individuals have developed a method of examining environmental issues that act as new demands or threats to the firm. The method involves two major analyses: the first examines the correlation and inten-

Exhibit 5
Worksheet for Environmental Opportunities and Constraints

ENVIRONMENTAL

Opportunities	Constraints

sity of demands made on the firm from sectors in the environment; the
second is the formulation of an Issues Alert System Matrix. Each of these
are shown in Exhibits 6 and 7. Let's briefly discuss each analysis.

Note that in Exhibit 6 we attempt to identify the extent to which the
major groups in the environment agree on major issues affecting our
firm. The top part of the figure is a scale of low to high which measures
the extent of agreement or correlation we think exists on issues that
affect us. The right-hand scale measures the degree of intensity or diffu-

Exhibit 6
Worksheet for Identifying Correlation and Intensity of Constituent Interest

CONSTITUENCY INTEREST CORRELATION

low	(Agreement/Correlation)	high

Exhibit 7
Worksheet for Issues Alert System Matrix to Prioritize Environmental Issues

IMPACT ON FIRM

	High	Medium	Low
High Priority			High
	Medium Priority		Medium
		Low Priority	Low

PROBABILITY OF OCCURRENCE

sion on a low or high basis that we think exists on any one particular issue. From our environmental analysis, we would place issues that we have identified into one of the four blocks in the figure.

Let's work through a couple of examples to see how this analysis works. Suppose we operate a paper mill. After we complete an environmental analysis, we note that there seems to be some pressure building to reduce or eliminate the odors that come from our mills. We note the following facts: local communities where our mills are located are considering odor control legislation, a federal law is under consideration, local citizens have demonstrated in front of some of our plants, our competitors have begun to reduce their odors, and technology is now available to clean up odors. We also note that feelings on this issue tend to run strongly—they are intensely held. We would then place this issue in the upper right-hand square since there seems to be high agreement or correlation among environmental groups on this issue and the feelings seem to be strongly held.

On the other hand, suppose we see an issue that is raised by only one or two constituent groups in the environment and that it is only raised on a casual basis (e.g., better landscaping around our paper plants). We would place this issue in the lower left-hand box.

The use of this framework helps us to classify better those environmental factors with which we must deal so we can begin to prioritize them. Once again, it helps us to deal with the issue of environmental overload. We can take the information from Exhibit 6 and plug it into Exhibit 7 to actually determine a priority. This Issues Alert System Matrix requires us to estimate the degree of impact of the issue on our firm and the probability that the issue will have an impact. Those issues with a high probability of having a great impact (upper left-hand box) would have the highest priority for us to address in the rest of the planning process. Those with the lowest probability of having a minor impact would receive relatively little attention from us in the planning process. Of course, we must be careful that an issue that we place in the lower right-hand box is correctly placed and that it does not creep up to the upper left-hand box without our knowing or explicitly acknowledging it.

At this point, we are now ready to extend this analysis to actually preparing an environmental forecast. We build on the information we generated in the environmental analysis to do this.

4.

Environmental Forecast

In this chapter, we build on the environmental analysis. In constructing the environmental analysis, companies often discuss various environmental trends. However, we are concerned with formalizing these trends for planning purposes.

Any environmental forecast is nothing more than an educated guess. Even those firms that spend considerable sums of money on building a forecast still are not able to achieve certainty. The idea behind the forecast is to reduce uncertainty and hence risk, as much as possible. It is pointless to postpone indefinitely the remaining steps in the strategic planning process because we want to reduce uncertainty to near zero. The cost of trying to do this and the added delays are not worth it. We should prepare a careful and thorough analysis and be willing to go with it. To do otherwise is to suffer from "analysis paralysis."

HOW IS AN ENVIRONMENTAL FORECAST CONSTRUCTED?

Final preparation of the forecast should rest with those doing the strategic planning. These individuals can be aided by a planning staff in larger organizations and by outside sources of information and consultants regardless of the size of the organization.

The idea behind the environmental forecast is to identify existing trends in various environmental sectors and to speculate as to how these trends will continue during the planning period. Also, emerging trends should be identified.

In identifying trends, we usually look to what has happened in the past and construct either a straight-line trend line or a curvilinear one. This is fine as long as we are fairly confident that the factors causing the trend in the past will continue to affect it in the future. If this is not so, we will be extending false trend lines into the future. This is a significant problem in high-tech industries where conditions are changing so rapidly.

The best method for constructing an environmental trend for strategic planning is to use a group of educated people either within or outside our organization who have a good idea of what is going on in the environment. These people should be well read, especially with books that deal with the outside environment. Such books as Peter Drucker's *Managing in Turbulent Times,* John Naisbett's *Megatrends,* and Alvin Toffler's *The Third Wave* are recommended reading. It is at this point that a knowledgeable group facilitator can be very helpful in getting the group to think through their ideas as to what they believe will happen in the various environmental sectors.

Even though the environmental forecast will never be totally accurate, it is important that a sufficient amount of time be spent in constructing the forecast. One of the biggest barriers to effective strategic planning are unforeseen emergencies or surprises that cause us to manage by reaction or crisis. The better the job that we can do to forecast environmental events, the less chance we will be surprised by them.

How Does an Environmental Forecast Differ from a Scan?

We must use the scan for building the forecast. It is difficult to predict the future if we do not know where we are now. We need a basis for projection, and it is the scan that gives us this basis. This is why it is so important to understand properly our present environment before we begin to speculate about what our future environment will be.

Some organizations complete the forecast at the same time they prepare the scan. This is okay as long as they realize which statements are statements of what now exists in the environment and which ones are estimations of future events. Keeping the two straight is essential for proper planning. We do not want to confuse what might happen with what is happening.

What Areas Should Be Forecasted?

In general, we should prepare a forecast of the same environmental sectors for which we prepared a scan. Exhibit 8 is a worksheet for preparing an environmental forecast. The space allocated to each sector can vary depending on the importance of the sector to the particular organization doing the planning. Exhibit 9 presents an example of an environmental forecast for a medium-sized manufacturer of modular housing. Notice that certain elements of the environment are given more detailed analysis than others because of the nature of the business. A hospital, credit union, or retail clothing store might choose to devote more time to forecasting other aspects of the environment deemed more relevant to the particular operation.

In compiling your forecast, you may wish to quantify more of the information than shown in the example in Exhibit 9. This is fine except

Exhibit 8
Worksheet for Completing an Environmental Forecast

ENVIRONMENTAL SECTOR	FORECAST
Economy	
Competition	
Legal/Political	
Social	
Demographic	
Technology	
Labor Market	
Suppliers	

Exhibit 8 (Continued)

ENVIRONMENTAL SECTOR	FORECAST
Distributors	
Key Physical Resources	
International Conditions	
Transportation	
Energy Supplies	

that quantification usually takes more time. It can also give the illusion of finiteness and a degree of accuracy not intended. Some people get hung up on the numbers and forget the purpose of an environmental forecast and how it is to be used in the strategic planning process. For this reason, those wishing to use numbers throughout may wish to specify a range and may even wish to specify a confidence level. So, for example, the data presented in the economic forecast could be presented as follows for prime interest rates: 12 to 14 percent, 75 percent confidence; 20 percent confident above 14 percent; and 5 percent confident below 12 percent. This would convey the message that the forecasters actually believe the

Exhibit 9
Sample Forecast for Modular Home Manufacturer

Environmental Sector	Forecast
Economy	Prime interest rate increasing to 14 percent over next two years, then declining to 11 percent range for two-year period. Inflation increasing to 12 percent annual rate within 12 months and remaining at that level for 12 to 18 months. GNP increasing this year at 4 percent level then declining to 2 percent and 0 percent two years from now. Unemployment holding steady at 8 percent for 2 years then increasing to 9.5 percent for 1 to 2 years.
Competition	An increase in the number of competitors during the next 18 months then a shakeout with the smaller, less efficient ones falling off. More options, larger homes, at higher prices. More site work. More opportunity to buy lot rather than rent.
Legal/Political	Possibility of some rent-control legislation affecting lot rental in some states (e.g., Florida). More monitoring of hazardous chemicals and substances in factories by OSHA. Zoning law changes in key states (e.g., Arizona and California). More lenient regulations on transporting homes on highways.
Social	Increased acceptance of modular home as acceptable housing because of lower price and lower home maintenance. Increased acceptance of modular home parks in communities because of larger homes and improved landscaping. Greater desire for luxury in modular homes.
Demographic	Increase in sunbelt population states where modular homes sold. Increase in over 62 age group. Increase in first home buyer age group. Smaller families.
Technology	Greater use of automated assembly line manufacture, including robotics, automated staplers and nailers. More efficient hauling from plant to sites involving both trucking and rail. Project site maintenance technique from retailer to location site of home.
Labor Market	Difficulty in locating competent drivers to transport homes from factory to retailer. No anticipated problems hiring employees in factories.
Key Physical Resources	Some problem in obtaining resins in laminating process. PCV pipe may be in short supply by year end. May have to vacate Memphis plant within 2 years if interstate bypass re-routing occurs.

Exhibit 9 (Continued)

Environmental Sector	Forecast
Suppliers	Some continued difficulty with major lumber supplier near Columbia plant if output of plant continues to increase rapidly. Need to diversify lines of credit. Anticipate supplier of PCV pipe in Memphis to cease business operations under Chapter 11 bankruptcy.
Distributors	Likely to lose retailers in Camden, S.C., Marietta, Ga., and Baton Rouge, La. Some continued trouble with R&R Trucking in Arkansas.
Transportation	Difficulty in obtaining qualified drivers for truck hauling. Rate problems for rail shipping.
Energy Supplies	Major problem in obtaining fuel for plants and trucks if war in Mideast expands. Anticipate electrical costs throughout system to increase 8 percent per year.
International Conditions	Conditions in Mideast may disrupt negotiations with UAR on distribution and sales to that country. Sales to Mexico expected to increase moderately if present government re-elected.

rate will be a bit higher than the 14 percent. Appendix B presents an economic forecast for a large public utility.

Larger firms often get quite sophisticated in their forecasts. They use probability methods, statistical analysis, and computer software to generate a comprehensive and detailed forecast. This is fine since they have the staff to help with this endeavor. But the absence of such staff should not keep the organization from forecasting.

The availability of personal computers and data bases will enable even the small company to become more sophisticated with environmental forecasting in the future. For this reason, you may wish to consider quantifying as many variables as possible when preparing the forecast.

WHAT ARE SOME METHODS OF FORECASTING THE ENVIRONMENT?

We mentioned that trend line analysis is a common method used. This method simply extends the past trend into the future. If energy prices have been rising an average of 5 percent per year for the last four years, we could assume that they will increase at this rate into the future.

However, we may see a curvilinear trend. Because of a current over-supply of energy, we might forecast only a 2 percent price increase for each of the next two years and a 5 percent increase each for years three, four, and five. Trend line analysis is a very common method to construct a forecast. However, there are two additional methods that are becoming more common. Each of these methods involves pooling the judgment of experts. The two methods are nominal group technique (NGT) and the Delphi process.

Nominal Group Technique (NGT)

This is a way to structure the input of people developing the forecast. (It is also often used as a problem-solving technique.) It is especially useful to overcome the reluctance of some people to provide opinions in group settings. The technique generates independent views and a great-er degree of meaningful participation. It can be used with the strategic planning group either in the planning workshop or outside of it. It can also be used with subcommittees of the group or with staff or line man-agement groups helping to formulate the forecast.

The basic steps in the process are as follows:

Step 1. Identify those who are to be involved in constructing the forecast (e.g., planning group, staff experts, line managers, committees, etc.). Set a three-hour meeting of this group.

Step 2. The group facilitator stands at the front of the room with a flip chart and writes out the item to be forecasted (or problem to be analyzed if it is used as a problem-solving technique). Example: How are social trends that affect our products/services changing during the next five years?

Step 3. Silent generation of ideas. Each person in the group writes down three major responses to the problem.

Step 4. In a round-robin fashion each person reads one item from his or her list. The facilitator records the item on the flip chart for all to see. There is no discussion of items at this time. This continues until each person's list is exhausted.

Step 5. Discuss the list of items on the chart. Allow clarification, support, and disagreement. Combine similar responses as appropriate.

Step 6. Each member ranks the items in writing in terms of their likelihood of occurrence. A scale of 1 to 5 or 1 to 10 could be used with the higher number being the most likely occurrence.

Step 7. The facilitator tabulates the results and selects those items that have some consensus. These are then discussed further.

Step 8. These are then incorporated into the environmental forecast.

This method is an excellent way to structure pooled opinions of experts and to allow everyone to have their say without one or two vocal people dominating the discussion.

The Delphi Method

This is another way to obtain structured responses from a group of experts to construct a forecast or to solve a problem. The difference is that it is used with people who are geographically dispersed over a fairly wide area and cannot readily get together for a face-to-face meeting. It is similar in some respects to NGT and can be used with the planning group, staff people, and outside experts in the field. The procedure is as follows:

Step 1. Identify the issue to be forecasted. State the issue to be examined. Example: What are the key changes in technology that will likely affect our operations during the next five years?

Step 2. Select the experts to be surveyed. Those surveyed should know something about the specific topic.

Step 3. Identify future states of nature that may influence forecasts. This should be briefly summarized and sent in a letter with the problem or key question to be forecasted. For example, we might indicate that technology could be stagnating, changing moderately, or changing rapidly with a brief (one-half page) description of each alternative state.

Step 4. Ask the experts to attach a probability to each state of nature as well as to provide opinions on each state and the specific technological changes envisioned. (This is done in the mailing.)

Step 5. Summarize, list, and assign a value of relative importance on the returned mailed responses from the experts using a 1 to 5 or 1 to 10 scale with the higher number being the more valuable expert. This rating should be done on the reputation and expertise of the particular expert rather than on whether the expert's opinion agrees with the opinion of the planning coordinator or consultant conducting the survey.

Step 6. Remail the most highly rated list of responses and ask each expert to evaluate each response including their opinion as to its likelihood of occurrence.

Step 7. Tabulate this final list of responses and incorporate into the forecast.

The Delphi Method is an excellent way to structure expert opinion from a geographically dispersed group. In a firm with several scattered locations or one that wishes to use outside experts in formulating its forecast, the method is an efficient way to structure responses.

We are now ready to consider the customer and market for our product and services.

5.

Customer/Market Analysis

Now we are ready to examine perhaps the most important part of our outside environment: our customer. The customer may go by a different name in your organization, as we see below, but the intent in this chapter is to ensure that we explicitly consider the people we intend to serve during the strategic planning process.

HOW SHOULD THE CUSTOMER BE DEFINED?

The customer is the person who buys our product or service. The consumer is the one who uses the product. Sometimes they are one and the same: a person buys a dinner at a restaurant and consumes it. However, they are often two different people: a mother buys clothing for her children. Every organization should understand who their customers and consumers are.

The customers and consumers make up the market for the firm's products and services. The organization may call these individuals by another name. For example, legal firms call their customers clients, doctors call theirs patients, schools call theirs students, credit unions call theirs members. Regardless of the specific terminology used, these individuals all have the primary characteristic of a consumer or customer— they are the recipients of the organization's products and services. Viewing them as customers connotes the necessity of meeting their needs and wants if we wish to maintain them as the lifeblood of the organization.

In this chapter, we do not provide a detailed analysis of the market as might be found in a marketing text. Rather, we look at the customer as the basis for developing a strategic plan. It is important that every organization thoroughly understand its customer before it begins formalizing its strategic plan. After all, the customer provides the ultimate justification for the existence of any organization. Any organization that fails to fulfill customer needs will eventually cease to exist in a competitive marketplace. Thomas Peters and Robert Waterman, in their best-selling management book, *In Search of Excellence,* list being customer driven as a key factor for a successful company. Zayre Corp., following this principle, has been able to formulate a successful and profitable strategy of marketing to minorities in inner-city areas avoided or abandoned by other major retailers. (See Johnnie L. Roberts, "Zayre's Strategy of Ethnic Merchandising Proves to Be Successful in Inner-City Stores," *Wall Street Journal,* September 25, 1984, p. 31.)

WHAT ARE IMPORTANT CUSTOMER CHARACTERISTICS?

Any listing of important customer characteristics to examine for planning purposes will vary depending on the business of the firm. However, most organizations will want to examine two broad categories of data: demographic information and psychological information. Let's look at each of these.

Demographic Information. Here we are interested in such factors as mean income, age, educational levels, geographic location, family size, and other factors that describe our customer. If our products and services appeal to more than one market segment, then we need to describe each segment. For example, General Motors offers a number of different automobiles that are targeted to different market segments.

Psychological Factors. Here we are interested in the particular needs and wants our products and services satisfy. Why do people buy our product or service over a competitor's? Usually, there are a number of needs that are being fulfilled. For example, people buy a new car not only because it provides a means of transportation, but also because it provides status, prestige, safety, security, and may create an image desired by the customer. In addition to the above needs, products may also satisfy some of the following needs: newness, intelligence, acceptance, innovativeness, practicality, convenience, economy, and sexual desirability. This is by no means a complete listing but rather is illustrative of the type of needs a product can satisfy. The point is that every organization must understand both the demographics and psychological factors of the market if it is to do a good job of strategic planning.

Exhibit 10 shows a workshop form that highlights the essential aspects of the market for planning purposes. Notice that we are emphasizing how the customer is changing over time. In strategic planning, we are concerned with satisfying the customer of tomorrow, not the customer of today or yesterday. Too often we are offering products and services based on historical information about our market that may not be valid for the future. We want to be sure that we will be able to satisfy the customer we will be serving next year, the year after, the year after that, and so on into the future.

HOW CAN WE PROJECT GROWTH?

We also need to project the growth of our customer base. Some firms do this by projecting sales. This is important, but we are not concerned with this at this point; rather, what we want to do here is to project a market base that we can target for a sales effort. In doing this we want to be sure to examine our competitor's market to determine if we can serve these customers better. The analysis we did previously of our competition should help us here. We also need to consider the effects that population growth and net migration will have on our market. We need to consider any new products or services that we are contemplating adding when we do this growth projection. If our product sales are directly dependent on the sales of another product, we need to forecast the sales of that product. For example, the sales of sheet steel are heavily dependent on the sales of automobiles. Forecasting auto sales would be an important part of forecasting market growth of sheet steel as would the determination of the amount of sheet steel used in each car. Obviously, smaller cars use less steel than larger cars.

When we project market growth, we are forecasting how much our market is projected to grow. If we project growth at 10 percent and we have a 20 percent share of the market which we intend to maintain, then our sales will grow by a proportionate amount. However, we may wish to change our market share or add new markets. Let's look at the four key factors to examine in market growth.

Growth of Existing Markets. This is simply a projection as to how much we think our existing market will grow. Unless we have 100 percent of the market, our sales will have a market share. Growth comes about here if we can at least maintain our share of the market as the market grows. If our share percentage falls faster than the market grows, we will lose sales. If the market is stagnating and our share falls, we will lose sales. Therefore, in a growing market, we would hope to at least maintain our market share.

Growth from Competitor Markets. Here, we want to take business away from competition. Our market may or may not be growing but we want to increase our market share. We want people to buy more Chrysler products and fewer Chevys, Fords, and Datsuns. Our projections in market growth by increasing market share by aggressively taking business from competitors would be reflected here.

Growth by Adding Markets. Here we would try to add markets for our product or service. We could expand geographically. We might find a substitute use for our product (e.g., baking soda as a refrigerator de-

Exhibit 10
Worksheet Form for Customer Analysis

CUSTOMER PROFILE

	Yesterday	Today	Tomorrow
Demographic			
Age:			
Income:			
Education:			
Geographic:			
Family Size:			
Other:			
Psychological			
Needs:			
Wants:			

PROJECTED
MARKET GROWTH

Existing markets:

New markets:

Competitor markets:

Other factors:

odorizer as well as for baking) or we might develop new products or services to serve new markets. We could also acquire existing companies and their markets and grow this way.

Other Factors Affecting Growth. There are several other factors to consider when forecasting growth.

* *Population trends.* Some products are very population sensitive. Baby foods and nursing homes are two common ones cited.

* *Growth philosophy.* Some companies don't wish to grow. Even though they might project market growth, they may believe smaller is better. They reason that a "lean, mean, fighting machine" is better able to survive a recession than would a fat conglomerate. After a period of rapid growth, some air carriers began to pare their operations in 1984 in order to survive in a deregulated environment. Other companies are divesting themselves of acquisitions made in the late seventies in order to survive the current times. Witness the rate of ITT divestitures in the mid-1980s. Some small family-held firms do not wish to grow much for fear of losing family control or of looking too attractive to an outside investor. The desire for control is a strong philosophy that affects growth. Of course, other firms wish to be a growth leader. They wish to grow as fast as possible to dominate a market. IBM adopted this approach once it entered the personal computer market. Chrysler under Lee Iaccoca has adopted this approach.

* *Economic conditions.* Our economic forecast is likely to have a major impact on our projected market growth. During boom times most markets grow. However, we should not be deceived by high levels of inflation that make it appear that our markets are growing when they are not. Prices are simply going up.

* *Managing growth.* A company can grow too fast. It can outstrip its management capability. Air Florida, Baldwin United, and Braniff are perfect examples of firms that grew far faster than the capability of the people to manage them. This factor should be examined to determine projected growth of sales.

* *State of technology.* Growth often comes about because of technological change. Witness the explosion in television broadcasting because of the advent of satellites and receiving dishes.

No doubt, other factors will influence growth depending upon the specific industry the organization finds itself in. These should also be examined.

WHAT IS THE ROLE OF CONSUMER AND MARKET RESEARCH?

Every organization must be concerned with doing market research. Even cities and counties are conducting resident opinion surveys to determine characteristics of the market. There are many ways to obtain market data. These include census data, hiring outside consultants to do the research, in-house staffing of a market research department, consumer panels or focus groups, buying market data through newsletters, and reviewing government studies. (These methods and others are discussed in the next section.) Most large organizations use a combination of these methods. Small organizations and those that do not sell to the ultimate consumer (i.e., industrial products companies) often do not use any structured method. Those companies that do not regularly monitor their market will have a difficult time surviving in the future.

Organizations that regularly gather market information will be able to complete this step in the planning process rather quickly. Those that have not done much market analysis in the past will find that they will have a considerable amount of work involved here to complete this step in the process.

WHAT ARE SOME WAYS TO LEARN ABOUT THE CUSTOMER?

There are a number of ways to learn about the customer. Each of these is briefly discussed below.

Census and Other Public Data and Information. The U.S. government provides a great deal of information on a host of markets. This not only includes census data on numerous factors by location, but also extensive analyses on various industries such as maritime, agriculture, steel, autos, and so on. These are available in most major libraries, such as university libraries, or can be acquired from the Superintendent of Documents, Washington, D.C.

Also trade and professional associations gather and publish material about markets. Various other organizations also publish such information, such as Predigast and Commerce Clearing House. Specific information about individual companies is published by Moody's, Standard & Poor's, and Dun's. This information is also usually available at most major libraries, especially those at universities with business schools.

Using Market Research Consultants. There are many companies that specialize in conducting market and consumer research for firms. This is also a fruitful way to learn about your market. Some of these firms use a survey and are quite sophisticated in tabulating the responses to the survey. They use many cross tabulations and correlations to give a pretty accurate and complete profile of customers and markets. A carefully selected market research consultant is especially useful for a small to medium-sized firm that cannot afford a full-time staff in this area.

In-House Market Research Department. Larger organizations can afford to have their own market research unit who regularly monitor the customer and the market. They may do periodic questionnaires, run test markets, evaluate promotional campaigns, interview selected customers as well as non-customers, and otherwise learn about the market.

Consumer Panels or Focus Groups. This method can be used by not only the large firm but also by the smallest. A representative sample of customers (and perhaps non-customers) meet to discuss the firm's products and services. If the group is properly structured and run, it can be extremely useful. Here are some guidelines:

- Select a panel representative of the entire customer base. You may also wish to include a few non-customers as part of the panel. The panel should not exceed 20 to 25 people.
- Select people who are willing and able to open up. They should be comfortable expressing their opinions in group settings.
- Have the group meet at convenient times and either pay them directly or give them discounts or free samples of company products and services or do both. Make them feel important. Give them the status and prestige they deserve.
- Ask them specific questions. Examples: What do you like best about our product? Why do you buy our product and not our competitor's? If you do not buy our product, why not? How do you use our product? Are you satisfied with the dealers who handle our product? How can we improve our product?
- Report back to them at their regular meetings as to how their ideas are being used. Let them know they are having an impact.
- Rotate membership on the panel every year or so to get new ideas.

Consumer Complaints or Hotline Calls. By monitoring consumer complaints and/or calls on our 800 hotline number (if we have one), we can get a reading on what problems customers are having with our product. This could lead to a better understanding of the needs and wants of our customers.

Getting Dealer Feedback. We can regularly quiz our dealers about our customers by asking dealers about the purchase behavior of people buying the product.

Compiling Warranty Registration Information. If we use a warranty registration card to be completed by the customer after purchase, we need to be sure we regularly compile and analyze the information and have it available for planning purposes.

Feedback from Our Salesforce. Our sales people deal with customers on a regular basis. We need to encourage and monitor feedback from our salesforce as to customer behavior, needs, and wants.

Employee Suggestions. Employees besides our salesforce may have excellent suggestions about the customer who uses our product. We can convene a panel of employees periodically and ask them to act as a consumer, forcing the panel to give us their ideas on customer profiles.

Customer Observation. Depending on our product, we might be able to unobtrusively observe our customer using it. For example, if we own a chain of motels, we can systematically observe customers checking into and out of the motel as an aid in forming a customer profile. If we own a bank, we could do the same observations at the teller windows. If we sell office computers, we could observe how they are used by our customers.

Therefore, there are many ways to obtain information about our customer in order to build a customer profile. It is essential that we gather as much information as we can. The needs of our customer should be the basis of all of our planning efforts.

Based on our analysis up to this point, we are now ready to specify the basic planning premises and key assumptions on which we will build our strategic plan.

6.

Strategic Planning Premises and Assumptions

If we have done a good job of examining our environment and market, we are then ready to make explicit our planning premises and assumptions. Planning premises and assumptions are our estimations about what the future holds. They are based on our environmental forecast. For example, if we forecast that the prime interest rate will increase to 14 percent as we did in the mobile home manufacturer example in Chapter 4, then a key planning premise for us would be that bank financing will be more difficult for us to obtain and that which would be obtained would be at a high rate. This would have significant implications for our cost of capital and other costs of doing business. These increasing costs would likely cut our profit margins.

WHAT IS THE ROLE OF A STRATEGIC PREMISE AND ASSUMPTION?

As we can see in the above example, strategic premises and assumptions help us to determine the implications of forecasted environmental events. They are a way for us to make explicit the impact the environment will likely have on our operations. They also make it clear what we see as assumption and what we believe to be fact. We use these strategic premises and key assumptions as the foundation for building our plan. Finally, we use these as a means to build planning scenarios.

WHAT ARE SCENARIOS AND HOW ARE THEY BUILT?

Scenarios are anticipated sequences of events that we believe may happen in the future. They specify a chain of events that will likely occur if something in the environment occurs. For example, if we predict that oil will increase in price by about 20 percent during the next two years, a scenario we might build might be as follows: fuel costs to run plants up 20 percent; total costs up 5 percent; price up 2 percent; sales down 8 percent; profits down 15 percent. In doing this, we are trying to trace through the effect of an environmental change on our operations. This serves then as a planning premise.

We might even develop alternative, competing scenarios to the one above. Then we could assign probabilities of occurrence to each scenario. Thus, we would be engaging in contingency planning, or planning for alternative futures. There is some value to doing this in that it forces us to anticipate what might happen that may be different from what we are actually planning for and to do something about it now before the events actually take place.

This process can become quite complicated, but the use of a personal computer and a software package such as Lotus 1- 2- 3 or Visicalc 1 or 2 can help with the spreadsheet analysis. We are likely to see more of this type of analysis as computer software becomes more sophisticated.

HOW ARE SPECIFIC PLANNING PREMISES AND ASSUMPTIONS FORMULATED?

Usually, planning premises and assumptions are built only for the most significant aspects of the outside environment and for the market.

Exhibit 11
Planning Premises for a Municipal Hospital

1. The anticipated cost control standards under medicare and medicaid will require us to control our fees and doctor charges more closely. Failure to do so will result in a substantial operating deficit.

2. Increased competition from the new private for-profit hospital and walk-in emergency facilities will require us to undertake an aggressive marketing effort to keep from losing paying patients at the expense of more indigents.

3. Significant improvements in medical and data-processing technology will place an increasing strain on our capital budget.

4. Population growth in the service area will place increasing strain on certain facilities that we have but that are not offered by competition (obstetrics, burn treatment center, pediatrics).

5. The nursing shortage will be exacerbated because of competition from other medical facilities driving up salaries by 20 percent during the next two years.

6. Energy cost increases will necessitate full implementation of energy cost control program in old wing.

7. Physician shortages in several key specialties will ease.

Exhibit 12
Worksheet for Planning Premises

PLANNING PREMISES (KEY ASSUMPTIONS)

1.

2.

3.

4.

5.

6.

7.

8.

This means that usually only 5 to 10 key premises or assumptions are developed. Of these, only half may have detailed scenarios developed. At some point, the costs of planning begin to exceed the benefits. This point is different for each firm, but planners must be mindful of reaching this point. Remember to avoid analysis paralysis.

The process of developing these premises and assumptions usually involves a great deal of discussion among the members of the planning group. Frequent reference will be made to the environmental and market analysis. These analyses may even be revised during the discussion. At some point, the discussion will need to stop and a final list of premises and assumptions developed, even though everyone might not be happy with them.

Exhibit 11 shows an example list of planning premises for a hospital. Note their straightforwardness and brevity. Several scenarios were built from these premises. Exhibit 12 is a worksheet for developing planning premises. The key thing to remember when developing these premises is that we are making explicit the assumptions that underlie any planning process. They can be modified during the planning process as new information surfaces. It is important not to get hung up on these but to get something reasonable down and then go on. They can always be revisited later.

We are now ready to move to the next step in the process: the internal assessment. We need to know where we are now before we can plan where we want to go.

7.

Internal Assessment

Imagine how difficult it would be to plan a trip if you did not know where you were going to start from. Determining where we are now is the purpose of this step in the planning process. Once we know where we are now, it will be easier to plan where we want to go.

WHAT IS AN INTERNAL ASSESSMENT?

An internal assessment is an examination of the status of key areas of the organization. The areas examined usually include personnel, products, services, operations, physical facilities, and so on. Sometimes this assessment is called an organization audit, operations analysis, management audit or review, or organizational assessment. Even though each of these may have a slightly different focus, the major intent is the same as an internal assessment.

Usually, when conducting the assessment, we want to identify the strengths and weaknesses of each of the key internal areas. We do this so that we can build objectives that overcome the weaknesses or problem areas while capitalizing on our strengths. This helps us to prioritize our objectives so that we can get the maximum return for the effort expended.

In conducting the assessment, recognizing when we have a problem is critical to our analysis. We will discuss some ways of surfacing and describing problems in a later section of this chapter, but one helpful idea to keep in mind throughout this analysis is the use of a desirable role model. This would be a comparable organization that has qualities we desire to emulate. For example, an autocratically run company may pick a company known for its participative management techniques, such as Motorola, 3M, Quasar, or Lincoln Electric, as a model to follow in assessing where they stand. Pointing to how relevant others do things helps us to determine if we have a problem. This is why the previous analysis of our competition is so important. So we need a basis for comparison if we are to do an adequate assessment.

We also need to examine problems we have been experiencing in a particular area. For example, if we are always having equipment breakdowns, we should gather the data on these (e.g., downtime, repair costs, lost production, etc.) and include these data in our assessment. Any problem that has been requiring a lot of attention should be included.

WHAT FACTORS ARE ASSESSED?

Exhibit 13 is a worksheet that shows the factors that are typically assessed. These factors can vary depending on the particular operations of the organization. Notice that all of these factors are internal to the organization. We should have already completed an assessment of factors external to the organization. Only a brief judgmental overall assessment of the strengths and weaknesses of each factor need appear on this worksheet. The data and other information to support the evaluation should appear in other reports or in appendices to the planning document.

HOW CAN THE ASSESSMENT BE DONE?

There are a number of ways to perform the assessment, ranging from an informal discussion among the planners concerning each area of the organization to quite sophisticated studies of the organization involving outside consultants. In this section we examine some of the methods which can be used.

Workshops

Almost always determination of strengths and weaknesses occurs through workshops. This occurs even when the organization uses sophisticated studies to gather data and other information for review. A thorough discussion of the strengths and weaknesses of the organization by the planners is important to help crystalize the direction of the strategic plan.

At these workshops, it is important that the participants feel free to express their opinions honestly. Keeping important information hidden for fear of hurting someone's feelings is not appropriate. These concerns should be raised in a tactful, straightforward manner. One purpose of strategic planning is to bring problems to the surface that for one reason or another have not surfaced before even though they have existed for quite some time. The use of an experienced group facilitator can be quite helpful here.

Exhibit 13
Worksheet for Internal Assessment

INTERNAL ASSESSMENT:
STRENGTHS AND WEAKNESSES OF (YOUR ORGANIZATION)

	STRENGTHS	WEAKNESSES
Personnel		
Products		
Operations		
Finances		
Physical Facilities		
Equipment		
Location		
Management		
Research and Development		
Customer Services/Image		
Special Assets/ Problems		
Other		

Data Gathering

Even though the workshop is an excellent way to finalize the assessment, almost always it will be necessary to gather data prior to the workshop. One way to do this is to use Survey Feedback. The Survey Research Center at the University of Michigan has a standardized instrument that can be purchased for this purpose. However, we present two instruments that have been used with a number of organizations both in business and the not-for-profit sectors.

The first instrument presented in Exhibit 14 is for use in smaller organizations. It is usually administered in a face-to-face interview conducted by an outside consultant or someone in the organization skilled in interview techniques. The advantage of this approach is that it provides the respondent with maximum flexibility for response and allows the interviewer to probe some areas in more depth. The disadvantages of this approach is that it is time consuming both to administer and tabulate, anonymity is not possible, and there may be some problem comparing responses from one person or one unit to the next.

Exhibit 15 shows a form that can be used in larger organizations. This form overcomes most of the objections of the essay form above, but it does restrict the respondent's answers. Of course, it is possible to use a combination of both forms or to design your own form. The point to keep in mind is that you want a form that solicits an honest response without biasing the respondent.

Another method to gather data is to use focus groups. These were originally developed as a way to analyze a firm's customers. Now they are also being used as a way to solicit employee opinions. They can be used with operative employees, supervisors, and middle management. Basically, a group of 15 to 20 people who represent various areas of the organization are brought together periodically (e.g., bimonthly) to discuss various areas of organizational operation. These groups are similar to a quality circle in the way they function, but they are more concerned with making evaluative judgments than are quality circles. Specific organizational problems are brought to the surface by the group. The parameters of the problem and possible solutions are prepared for management. When using this information for the organizational assessment, the planners should review the problems that have been addressed over the past year or two and determine to what extent they still exist. If quality circles exist in the organization, the results of their deliberations also should be reviewed.

Another much longer form for organizational assessment is presented in Appendix A. This assessment questionnaire is comprehensive and covers just about every aspect of organizational operation. If the organi-

Exhibit 14
Worksheet Questions for Survey Feedback Instrument in Smaller Organizations

---

SURVEY FEEDBACK INSTRUMENT IN SMALLER ORGANIZATIONS

1. What do you believe to be the three most important problems faced by your unit? Do you feel that you can do anything to solve these problems?

2. What do you believe to be the three most important problems faced by your organization? Do you feel that you can do anything to solve these problems? Why or why not?

3. If you were your unit's boss, which issues would you address first and why?

4. If you were the CEO, what issues would you address first and why?

5. What do you believe is the greatest managerial weakness of your unit and of your organization?

6. What other units in your organization cause your unit problems and what is the nature of these problems?

7. What time pressures do you experience on your job?

8. What has been your greatest disappointment since joining the organization?

9. What has been your most significant accomplishment since joining the organization?

10. Other comments?

Reprinted, by permission of the Publisher, from MANAGING INCOMPETENCE by William P. Anthony, © 1981, AMACOM, a division of American Management Associations. All right reserved.

zation has grown quite rapidly or if an assessment has never been done, the use of this form should be considered. This form could be addressed by the strategic planning group or could be administered to a sample of organizational employees. The results of the form will likely create quite a bit of discussion during the planning workshop.

Product/Service Analysis

The Boston Consulting Group has developed a model that can be used to analyze the product/service offering of a multiproduct/service organization. This matrix analyzes the product/service offering in terms of

Exhibit 15
Worksheet Questions for Survey Feedback Instrument
in Larger Organizations

1. Rank in priority the five most important problems faced by your unit from the following list. (Number them 1, 2, 3, 4, and 5. If less than 5, number only those that you feel apply.)
    _____ a. Lack of clear-cut goals.
    _____ b. Poor performance appraisal system.
    _____ c. Poor communications.
    _____ d. Too much employee turnover.
    _____ e. Inability to cope with change.
    _____ f. Outdated technology.
    _____ g. Shortage of staff.
    _____ h. Too many reports to complete.
    _____ i. Inability to achieve goals.
    _____ j. Budget is too limited.
    _____ k. Poorly trained and motivated employees.
    _____ l. General incompetence of managers.
    _____ m. Other (please specify) _____
    Do you feel you can help to solve these problems? _____

2. Rank in priority the five most important problems faced by your entire organization from the following list. (Number them 1, 2, 3, 4, and 5. If less than 5, number only those that you feel apply.)
    _____ a. Poor community/industry image.
    _____ b. Outdated product/service offering.
    _____ c. Outdated technology.
    _____ d. Lack of clear statement of organizational mission and goals.
    _____ e. Poor communication.
    _____ f. Declining industry
    _____ g. Lack of direction from the top.
    _____ h. Inadequate financial base.
    _____ i. Poor relations with regulatory agencies.
    _____ j. Poor customer/client relations.
    _____ k. Poor stockholder relations.
    _____ l. Poor profitability.
    _____ m. Lack of growth; stagnation.
    _____ n. Other (please specify) _____
    Do you feel that you can do anything about these problems? _____

3. If you were your unit's boss, which issues(s) listed in question 1 above would you address first, second, third? (1)_____,
    (2)_____, (3)_____.

4. If you were the CEO, which issues from question 2 above would you address first, second, and third? (1)_____,
    (2)_____, (3)_____.

5. Rank in order of priority the five most important management weaknesses in your unit and organization.

Exhibit 15 (Continued)

Unit		Weakness	Organization
_____	a.	Poor planning	_____
_____	b.	Lack of clear goals	_____
_____	c.	Poor leadership	_____
_____	d.	General incompetence	_____
_____	e.	Poor communications	_____
_____	f.	Poor placement of managers	_____
_____	g.	Little positive rewards	_____
_____	h.	Poor management of time	_____
_____	i.	Lack of vision	_____
_____	j.	Inability to deal with change	_____
_____	k.	Poor management controls	_____
_____	l.	Out of touch with lower levels in organization	_____
_____	m.	Inability to coordinate activities across units	_____
_____	n.	Other (please specify):	_____

6. What other organization units cause your unit the most problems?
   a. _____
   b. _____
   c. _____
   d. _____

7. Indicate the time pressures faced in your job (check all that apply).
   _____ Can't yet my work done in eight hours a day.
   _____ Not given enough notice on major projects.
   _____ Can't complete reports on time.
   _____ Meetings take up too much time.
   _____ Emergencies always coming up.
   _____ Not enough good people to delegate to.
   _____ Too much correspondence to answer.
   _____ Too many daily interruptions.
   _____ Can't return phone calls in a timely manner.
   _____ Not enough time for personal/professional development.
   _____ Have to work at odd hours (nights, weekends, holidays).
   _____ Other (please specify) _____

8. What has been your most significant accomplishment since joining the organization? _____

9. What has been your greatest disappointment since joining the organization? _____

10. Other comments?

whether the product/service falls into one of four cells shown in Exhibit 16. To determine where each product/service falls, the growth rate of the industry where the product competes and its relative market share are determined. Based on these two criteria, the products/services are placed into these cells:

Stars: High business growth rate and strong relative market or competitive position

Cash Cows: Slow business growth rate and strong relative market or competitive position

Exhibit 16
The Boston Consulting Group Portfolio Matrix for Classifying Products/ Services

RELATIVE COMPETITIVE POSITION

	strong	weak
high	STARS	QUESTION MARKS
low	CASH COWS	DOGS

BUSINESS GROWTH RATE

Question Marks: High business growth rate and weak relative market or competitive position

Dogs: Slow business growth rate and weak relative market or competitive position

Once the products/services are placed into one of the four cells, the next step is to analyze the future position of each product/service. For example, for the stars, the key objectives should be to maintain market share with current profitability given a lower priority. For the cash cows, the idea would be to maximize current profitability since market growth rate is so slow. For the question marks, efforts should be focused on expanding market share where possible since a high growth market exists. Finally, for the dogs, consideration should be given to dropping the product or service.

This matrix is not without its limitations. For example, there are other factors to consider when viewing the attractiveness of an industry besides growth rate, and there are no middle cells for the "average position." Yet the matrix does have some value for providing a systematic evaluation of an organization's product/service offering. It certainly will encourage a lot of discussion among the strategic planners, especially when disagreements arise as to proper product placement.

Financial Analysis

The last area we examine from an assessment standpoint is the financial picture of the organization. Any strategic plan must be built on the basis of a thorough understanding of the financial health of the organization. In this section, we do not discuss a course in financial management or accounting. That task is beyond the scope of this book. Rather, we present the elements of a rather simple approach to financial analysis. This approach serves as a way to red flag areas that might need more in-depth analysis using the tools of the accountant or financial analyst.

The primary tools of financial analysis are ratios—proportions that relate one measure to another. Ratios are important because they permit comparative study in two distinct ways. First, they derive their importance by measuring historical trends within the organization itself. Changes in critical ratios may signal the existence of underlying financial problems that are yet to emerge.

Second, through information provided by trade publications, government business statistics, and private firms, such as Dun and Bradstreet, meaningful ratio comparisons can be made throughout the industry as a whole. These comparisons can supply important financial information by providing a standard by which to measure the firm's progress and by identifying changing trends within other firms and within the industry.

There are five basic types of financial ratios as shown in Exhibit 17: liquidity, activity, leverage, coverage, and profitability. The numbers in the parentheses in the ratios refer to the simplified balance sheet and income statement presented in Exhibit 18.

Liquidity ratios measure the ability of the firm to pay its short-term obligations. There are two primary liquidity ratios: the current ratio and the quick ratio.

The current ratio is measured by current assets divided by current liabilities. It indicates the extent to which short-term claims are covered by assets that will soon be cash. A general rule of thumb states that the current ratio should be from 2.0 to 2.5, but this can vary according to the industry. A current ratio that is relatively low may indicate a lack of liquidity, while a high ratio may show that investment in more permanent assets can be accomplished without a meaningful loss in liquidity.

The quick (or acid) ratio is measured by current assets less inventory divided by current liabilities. This ratio measures the ability of the firm to pay its short-term debt without relying on the sale of inventory. Again, a general rule of thumb states that the quick ratio should be 1.0 at minimum. Depending on how quickly the firm turns over its inventory, the quick ratio may be a better measure of short-term solvency than the current ratio.

A second group of ratios are known as activity ratios. These measure how effectively the firm is using its resources. Inventory turnover, average collection period, and total asset turnover are three major activity ratios.

The inventory turnover ratio is measured by sales divided by inventory. This ratio measures the number of times inventory is sold during the year and the speed to which inventory is converted to cash. This ratio should be used in conjunction with the liquidity ratios mentioned earlier.

The average collection is measured as accounts receivable divided by sales, which are divided by 360. It measures the average number of days collectibles are outstanding and is a reflection of the firm's credit policy. This ratio should be viewed on an historical basis, since lengthening collection periods may indicate the need to tighten credit policies.

The total asset turnover ratio is measured by sales divided by total assets. This ratio measures how efficiently the firm is using its capital resources to generate sales dollars. A declining total asset turnover ratio may be an indication of falling efficiency.

A third group of ratios are leverage ratios, which measure the extent to which the firm is financed by debt. The major leverage ratios are the debt ratio and debt-to-equity ratio.

The debt ratio is measured by total debt divided by total assets. The debt ratio measures a firm's leverage, the percentage of its total assets financed by the firm's creditors. An increasing ratio is indicative of growing risk, but overall risk should be viewed in relation to industry norms.

The debt-to-equity ratio is long-term debt divided by owner's equity. This ratio measures the relationship between funds provided by creditors and by the firm's owners and is a reflection of the methods used by the firm to obtain funds. An increasing ratio demonstrates greater bor-

Exhibit 17
Ratios for Financial Analysis

LIQUIDITY RATIOS:

Current— $\dfrac{\text{Current Assets (11, 12, 13)}}{\text{Current Liabilities (16)}}$

Quick or Acid— $\dfrac{\text{Current Assets}-\text{Inventory (11, 12)}}{\text{Current Liabilities (16)}}$

ACTIVITY RATIOS:

Inventory Turnover— $\dfrac{\text{Sales (1)}}{\text{Inventory (13)}}$

Average Collection Period— $\dfrac{\text{Accounts Receivable (12)}}{\text{Sales/360 (1)}}$

Total Asset Turnover— $\dfrac{\text{Sales (1)}}{\text{Total Assets (15)}}$

LEVERAGE RATIOS:

Debt— $\dfrac{\text{Total Debt (16, 17)}}{\text{Total Assets (15)}}$

Debt-to-Equity— $\dfrac{\text{Long-term Debt (17)}}{\text{Owner's Equity (18, 19)}}$

COVERAGE RATIOS:

Times Interest Earned— $\dfrac{\text{Earnings before Interest and Taxes (6)}}{\text{Interest Expense (7)}}$

Fixed Charge Coverage— $\dfrac{\text{Earnings before Interest and Taxes (6)}}{\text{Fixed Charges (5, 7)}}$

PROFITABILITY RATIOS:

Profit Margin on Sales— $\dfrac{\text{Net Income (10)}}{\text{Sales (1)}}$

Return on Assets— $\dfrac{\text{Net Income (10)}}{\text{Total Assets (15)}}$

Return on Net Worth— $\dfrac{\text{Net Income (10)}}{\text{Total Equity (18, 19)}}$

Exhibit 18
Sample Financial Statements for Ratio Analysis

XYZ Company Income Statement
For the Year Ended December 31, 19X0

(1)	Sales	1,000
(2)	Cost of Goods Sold	(750)
(3)	Gross Margin on Sales	250
(4)	Selling and Administrative Expense	(40)
(5)	Leasing Expenses	(10)
(6)	Income before Interest and Taxes	200
(7)	Interest Expense	(10)
(8)	Income before Taxes	190
(9)	Income Tax Expense (50%)	(95)
(10)	Net Income	95

XYZ Company Balance Sheet
December 31, 19X0

(11)	Cash	50	(16)	Current Liabilities	100
(12)	Accounts Receivable	100	(17)	Long-term Liabilities	300
(13)	Inventory	100	(18)	Common Stock	400
(14)	Plant, Property,		(19)	Retained Earnings	200
	and Equipment	750			
(15)	Total Assets	1,000	(20)	Total Liabilities and	
				Equity	1,000

rowing and greater risk. Again, this should be used in conjunction with industry standards.

A fourth classification of ratios is known as coverage ratios. They measure the ability of the firm to pay its fixed financial costs. The two primary coverage ratios are the times interest earned ratio and the fixed charge ratio.

The times interest earned ratio is measured by earnings before interest and taxes divided by interest expense. This ratio measures the extent to which earnings may decline before the firm is unable to meet its contractual obligations. The higher the ratio, the more able the firm is to fulfill its required interest payments. As the ratio declines, the firm may begin to experience problems meeting these fixed payments.

The fixed charge coverage ratio is measured as earnings before interest and taxes divided by fixed charges (including payments on debt, lease payments, preferred stock dividends, etc.). It determines the ability of the firm to meet its fixed financial costs. As before, a declining ratio may signal future problems.

The final major group of ratios are profitability ratios, which measure the firm's effectiveness as shown by returns on sales and investment. Profit margin on sales, return on assets, and return on net worth are three major profitability ratios.

The profit margin on sales is measured as net income divided by sales. This ratio gives the profit margin per dollar of sales. As with other measures, it should be viewed in terms of trend and industry averages.

The return on assets is measured as net income divided by total assets. This ratio, also known as the return on investment, measures the return on total assets of the firm. At a minimum, it must be greater than the firm's effective interest rate, which is interest expense divided by total liabilities, if the firm is to survive in the long run.

The return on net worth is equal to net income divided by total equity. This ratio measures the rate of return on the owner's investment in the firm. Generally, the higher the return, the better off the owners are.

Ratios serve as a very useful tool of financial analysis, but a few words of caution are in order. First, in order to ensure comparability, use audited financial statements as the basis for the ratios. Also, be sure the dates of the statements are the same so that false conclusions from seasonality can be avoided. Check to make sure that a major change has not been made in the method of accounting from one statement to the next. For example, a switch in depreciation methods will give an inaccurate picture of certain ratios. Finally, use groups of ratios in the analysis; a single ratio does not provide sufficient information to judge the performance of the firm.

This concludes the assessment phase of the strategic planning process. This step is more comprehensive than previous steps because too often an organization builds a plan without having an accurate idea of what they are doing now. Since a plan involves moving forward from our present position, it is absolutely essential that we have an accurate reading on our present position. It is very difficult to set goals for the future if we do not know what we have accomplished in the past.

8.

Mission Development

We are now ready to determine the mission of our organization. Notice that we do not formally address this issue until we have looked at the outside environment, the market, and our internal operations. Most likely, as we discussed each of these areas, we would discuss elements of our mission. This is fine; but we should not formalize our mission until we have completed a thorough external and internal examination. It is only after we have completed this examination that we are accurately able to align ourselves with our market and environment by capitalizing on our strengths and taking advantage of environmental opportunities. We want to be sure that we are not so wedded to our present mission that we overlook important environmental opportunities. However, we do not want to try to be all things to all people so that we spread ourselves too thin.

WHAT IS A MISSION STATEMENT?

A mission statement sets out the overall purpose of the organization. It is an overriding or all-encompassing goal. It is the ultimate rationale for the existence of the organization. Often, the elements of a mission statement can be found in the corporate charter or other important corporate document. If the organization is a government agency, the mission or elements of it can be found in legislation creating the agency.

However, even though the elements of a mission statement can be found in an important document, it usually will be incomplete. Therefore, the mission statement should be thoroughly discussed during the strategic planning process.

The mission statement makes explicit the domain of the organization. The domain and domain consensus were discussed earlier in the section on the environment. It is at this point, however, that we really try to pin down what it is that the organization is really about.

WHAT ARE THE KEY ELEMENTS OF A MISSION STATEMENT?

There are nine key elements of a good mission statement. Each of these is discussed below.

Brevity. The mission statement for the organization should be fairly short; no more than a couple of paragraphs in length. Conciseness is important.

All-Encompassing. Even though brief, the mission statement should lay out the key purpose of the organization. Simply to say "to make money" is not enough. Presumably, every business organization has this as its purpose. However, as we see below, money should be addressed someplace in the mission statement.

Commitment to Economic Efficiency. If we are a private business, we should state someplace in our mission statement that we want to maximize profit to the extent possible given the constraints that we face. If we are a government or not-for-profit organization, we should make a commitment to economic efficiency and effectiveness. We should try not to waste money.

Broad Statement of Products/Services Offered. Our mission statement should indicate what line of business we are in. It is not necessary to list all of our products and services, but it is necessary to identify briefly the broad classes of our products and services. It is also important that we understand the industry we are in. For example, the Ace Trucking Co. could define its mission as being in either the trucking or the transportation industry. The difference is a major one: the trucking industry is much more narrow than the transportation industry. Such a narrow approach might very well limit the market and environmental opportunities for the company.

Market Served. The geographic market served should be included in the mission statement. Are we a local, state-wide, regional, national, or international company? What are our major market groups?

Continuing in Nature. Even though we may want to review our mission statement annually, we should be careful about making major changes in it. The mission statement should have an ongoing nature. It should last for about a 4- or 5-year period without any major changes. Of course, if an opportunity comes along or other major events occur, the statement may need to be changed. But this should only occur after very thorough discussion and analysis. This mission statement should serve as an anchoring device.

Unique or Distinctive in Some Way. The statement ought to tell how the organization is different from other organizations in the industry. This is where the modeling aspects come into play again. With what organizations do we wish to be compared? Do we wish to be viewed as an industry leader or follower? How are we different from our competitors?

Exhibit 19
Sample Mission Statements

Our mission is to show people how to become more self-sufficient—one of the most necessary qualities in a world of restricted, expensive resources.

Robert Rodale
Rodale Press

We believe that this University was created to offer the people of Florida high quality, comprehensive graduate programs grounded in basic research and nourished by strong professional programs of study. We believe that such a mission gives added distinction and quality to our fine undergraduate programs and our extensive public service outreach activities. We know that good teaching requires good research and vice versa.

Florida State University

The mission of the College of Business of the Pine Mountain State University is to provide efficiently and effectively graduate (including doctoral), undergraduate, and non-credit education in management and administrative sciences to students, primarily from Virginia, but also from other states and foreign countries. It also encompasses conducting research and publication, which results in publication and in providing professional service to the University, community, and profession.

College of Business Mission

Our mission is to apply our experience in our core business of telecommunications to other areas of information movement, both regulated and non-regulated, that offer high growth and profit potentials. We plan to continue with products/services in cellar mobile phone service, a new generation of communications systems for automated offices, advanced voice and data terminals, and, through a subsidiary, Bell Yellow Page directories.

Telecommunications Company

To provide efficiently and effectively up-to-date preventative and curative comprehensive health care services to the southeastern part of the state while maintaining a strong community image and an excellent reputation as a place to practice and work.

Private, Not-for-Profit Hospital

To become known as the best sailboard in the industry by providing a high quality product at a fair price backed by a strong dealer network. To consistently grow at a rate of at least 20 percent per year in both sales and profitability in order to become the dominant manufacturer in the industry. To seek out related product lines continually for product expansion.

Manufacturer of Leisure Products

Exhibit 20
Worksheet for Developing a Mission Statement

PURPOSE OR MISSION STATEMENT WORKSHEET

MISSION OR PURPOSE:

_____
_____
_____
_____
_____
_____
_____

Key factors to use in writing and evaluating a mission statement:
1. Brief
2. All-encompassing
3. Commitment to economic efficiency
4. Broad statement of products/services offered
5. Market served geographically
6. Continuing in nature
7. Unique or distinctive in some way
8. Consistent with unit missions
9. Understandable

Consistent with Unit Missions. We should be sure that the overall organization mission is consistent with the missions of subordinate units. Generally, the overall corporate mission is set before unit missions are set, but even after unit missions are set, we need to review all mission statements for consistency. It might be that certain facts surfaced during the setting of unit missions that will cause us to modify our corporate mission.

Of course, if we are a major subsidiary of a large conglomerate, we need to be sure that our mission dovetails with that of our parent organization.

Understandable. It should go without saying that a mission statement should be understandable, but unfortunately, some are written in such convoluted English and are so full of buzzwords and acronyms that they are virtually impossible to understand. Remember, the mission statement is a key part of the strategic planning process. It should be written to express, not impress.

Some examples of mission statements are presented in Exhibit 19. These are actual statements. Some are better than others. Exhibit 20 presents a worksheet for developing a mission statement. During a workshop, it may take anywhere from one to six hours to finalize a mission depending on the extent of disagreement among the planners and the amount of experience they have had in working with the mission.

9.

Strategic Thrusts or Key Goals

Strategic thrusts are the important or key goals that we wish to accomplish during the planning horizon. They are very high priority items and will set the basic direction of the organization for the strategic planning period. In this chapter, we review the meaning of strategic thrusts and the manner in which they are determined.

WHAT ARE STRATEGIC THRUSTS?

Strategic thrusts are major goals that set the basic directions of the organization and involve a major commitment of resources of the organization for the planning horizon. Once set, they are not easily changed. They reflect the way in which the organization capitalizes on its internal assets to take advantage of market opportunities. They give added meaning to the mission statement and evolve from that statement. They explicitly exploit the organization's advantages over the competition. They set the foundation for the development of more specific operational objectives. They are strategic in that they reflect a basic strategy the organization has adopted for carrying out its functions.

For example, a large credit union I once worked with developed a strategic thrust which read as follows: "To be as convenient for customer use as any other financial institution in the area and to meet or beat the loan and investment rates of any other financial institution in the area."

This strategic thrust reflects a strong competitive philosophy that is very different from the traditional philosophy of credit union management. It follows from a mission statement that implied that the credit union wished to be a full financial institution to compete directly with banks and savings and loan institutions. From this strategic thrust would flow a host of specific objectives and programs in such areas as hours of operation, location of branch offices, staffing of teller windows, drive-in facilities, automated teller machines, toll-free telephone calling, invest-ment programs, loan programs and policies, and cash management. The strategic thrust statements are like arrows that are shot into the future and pull the organization along.

Normally, the organization should write only three to five strategic thrust statements each planning period. During the planning period, as with all elements of the strategic plan, they can be revised as needed. The reason that they are kept to such a small number is to focus priorities. We can not be all things to all people, and the strategic thrust statements help us to focus our efforts. Some additional examples of strategic thrusts are provided in Exhibit 21.

Exhibit 21
Examples of Strategic Thrusts

We are internally oriented. We organized ourselves by functions. We must discard many of our internal service standards and become market oriented. The function needs to be in the other directions. The customer is king. Maybe the customer doesn't care about some of the things we thought he should care about. We need to find this out and we need to beat the competition in meeting the customer's needs.

President of a Large Trucking Firm

When we introduced our management accounts, we declared war on banks, savings and loans, and stock brokerage houses saying we are going to be the asset gatherers of our members. We're going to take the wealthy individual and the not-so-wealthy individual, and we're not going to be a traditional credit union runing operations out of a cigar box.

Manager of a Large Credit Union

We expect to be as convenient as any other financial institution in our market-ing area and to meet or beat the savings, investment, and loan interest rates of any financial institution in our market.

CEO of a Large Savings and Loan

We want to be the Harvard of the Midwest. When people think of quality graduate education in business we want them to think of us as well as Harvard, Stanford, or any other so-called prestigious business school.

Dean of a Midwestern School of Business

Though mainly a supplier to industry, especially companies in the chemical, petrochemical, and electronics fields, we are going to expand our consumer line. We will market a catalytic filter for kerosene heaters, a catalytic system for use in newer models of wood-burning stoves, and we will provide a variety of water filters for home use.

Manager of an Industrial Products Firm

Exhibit 21 (Continued)

Our researchers have plumbed the depths of the potential reader's psyche on every thing from where storis should be placed to how long they should run. Our planning committee wrestled with the data and developed a formula that would be the magazine's format. Market research is not new to the magazine business, but this is the first time market research has actually shaped the look and feel of a new magazine. The customer is king. We really do plan on giving our readers what they want.

Publisher of a New Magazine Venture

Through our commitment and teamwork, we plan on becoming America's premier export bank. Our export division is a leader in agricultural export credits, export trading companies, and countertrade. Last year alone, we financed almost a billion dollars of agricultural products to overseas markets, using CCC and FCIA programs. Through our trading company joint venture we're now offering many unique capabilities—such as origination of deals, search for buyers, marketing, shipping goods, arrangement of financing, and countertrade. We plan to continue this strategy in the future.

Vice President of a Large Bank

We hit the acquisition trail in the early seventies in an effort to widen the base of our dental products business, then consisting principally of the small nuts and bolts product. In 1970–1971, we added Style Right dental chairs. Then we added Dynamo x-ray equipment. By the late seventies, we had made other major acquisitions. By the end of this decade, we want to offer office furniture and other items for the dentist's office. We want to become the dentists's one stop place to shop to set up his office.

President of a Dental Equipment Supply House

We want to become America's largest transportation company. Our mergers have increased our assets to over $5 billion while adding trucking, shipping, and rail ventures around the world. We plan to add an airline firm, rental car company, and package handler in the next two years. If it moves, we want to ship it.

CEO of a Large Transportation Company

We want to be known as America's new, low-cost, no-frills airline. We want to provide the cheapest fares in the industry without compromising safety and on-time reliability. When people want to fly, we want them to think of us and no one else.

CEO of an Air Carrier

WHY ARE STRATEGIC THRUSTS IMPORTANT?

As indicated above, strategic thrusts help us to set priorities, focus our efforts, and aim our resources at a few very important targets. But they do more than this. Since they usually deal with new directions or a refocusing of present programs, they play an important communication role as well. They communicate to others outside the organization what we are all about and where we are going. They help our customers, investors, suppliers, distributors, and public interest groups understand our new directions. They also serve an important internal communication function. They help our managers set individual objectives and priorities. They serve as a rallying point for effort.

Notice the statements in Exhibit 21. They reflect major actions the organizations plan to take or are in the midst of taking. These statements reflect a proactive posture with respect to the environment and market. So often an organization will feel as if it is at the mercy of the market and environment. This is especially so of smaller firms, or when the environment is uncertain and ambiguous. This reactive posture is not appropriate from a strategic planning perspective. We must understand our environment, not so that we can knuckle under to it but so that we can actively capitalize on it given the constraints we face. This is really the message of environmental analysis. Unless we come up with clear-cut strategic thrusts, the environmental and market analysis is virtually useless.

However, the development of strategic thrusts is not the entire story. We must make these strategic thrusts operational. In Exhibit 21, only one strategic thrust for each organization represented was shown. Each organization no doubt has several other strategic thrusts. But for these to have meaning, operational objectives and a method for their achievement must be developed. That is the subject for the next four chapters.

Part II

Operationalizing the Strategic Plan

The second part of this book examines the ways to make a strategic plan come alive. Chapter 10 discusses how to develop and write achievable objectives. The next chapter describes how to develop action steps and schedules for each objective. This is so very important. If a strategic plan is to be fully implemented, it is very important that the plan be tied to a budgeting cycle; chapter 12 shows how to do so.

In chapter 13, the ways of tracking and measuring performance in achieving the plan are discussed. The last chapter in this part explains how to design systems for corrective action to redirect a strategic plan that is not developing as planned.

10.
Developing and Writing Objectives

In order for the strategic plan to become reality, it must be made operational. This means becoming quite specific about elements of the plan by dealing with the three basic questions: Who? Will do what? By when?

Answering these questions may not be the province of the strategic planning group; however, seeing that they do get answered is their responsibility. Since strategic planning is to be a participative process, it is at this point that middle- and lower-level managers get involved.

The steps involved in operationalizing the strategic plan are shown in Exhibit 22. This is a portion of Exhibit 1 presented in the first chapter of this book. This chapter deals with the first part of the process: developing and writing specific objectives.

HOW CAN OPERATIONAL OBJECTIVES BE DEVELOPED?

Specific objectives must flow from the strategic thrusts developed in the previous step and must be consistent with the mission of the organization. The manner in which these objectives are actually set can vary from rather autocratic to very participatory techniques, although the literature and research on the subject almost unanimously recommends some form of participation in order to gain commitment from those expected to achieve the objectives. Let's briefly look at some methods that can be used to set objectives.

Autocratic Announcement. Probably the worst way to set objectives is by autocratic announcement since most people resent being told what to do. However, it can buy short-term compliance at the expense of long-term commitment. If time is of the essence or if there is a true crisis, then unilateral setting of specific objectives by a higher-level group is acceptable. Of course, true time and emergency constraints must actually exist;

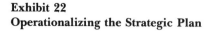

Exhibit 22
Operationalizing the Strategic Plan

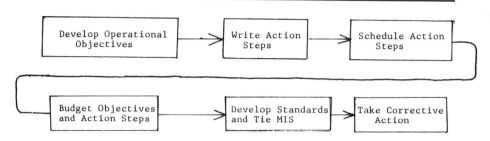

some managers cry emergency when none exists as an excuse for unilateral objective setting.

Consultive. With the consultive method, the subordinates at each level in
the organization are given the opportunity to have some input to the
objectives of their boss and their work group. They do not actually determine the objectives; they simply review those that have been set by their
boss and offer suggestions for modification. The boss is free to accept or
reject the suggestions. The problem with this approach is that it creates
expectations on the part of the subordinate that the opinions offered will
at least be considered and accepted. Often they are not.

Participative. The participative approach is most often recommended
because it gets the group involved and enhances the commitment of the
group to achieving the final objectives. It has its limitations: it is time
consuming, it requires open discussion, and the participants must want
to participate and have the knowledge to participate intelligently. However, most people who have studied the matter believe that the advantages of the approach outweigh the disadvantages.

There are several forms of participation. *Consensus* participation involves reaching general agreement among group members using compromise. The group considers various alternatives and modifications of
objectives and then generally agrees on a final list. The use of consensus
is common in some Japanese firms, especially in the electronics and
automobile industries. *Democratic* participation differs from consensus in
that formal votes on objectives are taken by the group. Motions are made
and seconded to accept or reject objectives and then the group votes on
them. The manager, who acts as the head of the group, usually has the
right to override the group vote under certain circumstances. For example, there may be a "home office" mandate that the group must accept or
a law may be involved that requires the group to accept an objective,
such as one on affirmative action or safety.

The final form of participation is *free reign* where the group actually
formulates the objectives with minimal leadership from the boss. It is as

if they formulate the objectives and announce them to the boss. This situation is rare except with professional groups such as research scientists, some university departments, some medical centers and legal firms, and some independent research centers.

HOW CAN PARTICIPATION BE ENHANCED IN SETTING OBJECTIVES?

Most groups use planning workshops such as those discussed in other parts of this book. A planning workshop, either on the job or away from the job in a retreat-like atmosphere, can be an excellent way to set specific objectives. One method to enhance the participation at these workshops is nominal group training (NGT) which we discussed as a method for forecasting. This method can be used with or without an outside consultant. The method works as follows when setting objectives:

1. A question is developed and presented to the group by the group facilitator involving an objective. The question should be stated in a problem format. Example: How can we improve quality control?
2. The question is presented on a flip chart to the group. Without discussing the question, each group member spends 5 to 10 minutes writing down ideas on a sheet of paper in front of them.
3. In round-robin fashion, each person presents one idea from his or her private list. Each idea is recorded on the flip chart at the time it is presented. There is still no discussion at this point.
4. Once everyone's list has been exhausted and all ideas have been recorded, the ideas are discussed by the group. Usually, the person presenting the idea begins the discussion of it.
5. After discussion, each member of the group lists by priority the three best ideas in their opinion. These votes are then tallied by the group facilitator.
6. The process continues on the top-rated ideas until just three or four are left. From this, an objective or two is developed.

The advantages of this approach are that it structures group participation, gives everyone a chance to have their say, keeps the discussion focused, and is easy to use. It also uses pooled voting as a technique to reach a consensus. However, it is time consuming and requires a group facilitator who will enforce the rules.

The Delphi technique also can be used when the participants are geographically dispersed since it works the same as NGT except that the development of lists and serial voting is done by mail. Of course, discussion of the ideas is not possible except that participants are given the opportunity to make brief comments about various ideas.

Even with these two techniques, the group facilitator plays a critical role in encouraging discussion during the work sessions. People should feel free to communicate openly about various objectives under consideration. The group facilitator must be careful to draw people out, not let certain individuals dominate the discussion, keep the discussion on target and moving along, and to summarize and record points as appropriate.

WHAT ARE THE CRITERIA FOR A GOOD OBJECTIVE?

While there is some debate on exactly what a good operational objective should look like, there is agreement on several important points. The criteria for a good objective are summarized in Exhibit 23.

It is important that each operational objective meet each of these criteria insofar as possible. The closer each objective meets these criteria, the easier it will be to track and measure their accomplishment. The tracking and measuring is critical to ensure that the objective actually gets accomplished. Usually, the most difficult criterion to meet is quantifiability. A worksheet for use in quantifying a difficult-to-quantify objective is presented in Exhibit 24. Finally, Exhibit 25 presents some sample objectives. Notice in this example how each objective ties into the strategic thrust at the top of the page.

WHY DO OBJECTIVES NEED A RATIONALE?

A rationale for each objective helps us to better understand why we have the objective in the first place. This rationale should relate to the strategic thrust, an identified problem to be corrected, an expected environmental opportunity or constraint, or a change in mission focus. There is some debate as to whether the specific rationale for each objective should be stated below the objective. Probably the best idea here is to state it only when there is likely to be some confusion on the part of those reading the objective as to why it is needed. If the reason is obvious, then there is little need to state it.

If the rationale is stated, it should be clear and concise. Here is an example:

Objective: To reduce employee turnover from 55 percent on an annual basis to 25 percent by December 31, 1985.

Rationale: Turnover in our production facilities has been increasing by about 10 percent per year for the last three years. We are now substantially above the 30 percent average rate in our industry.

Notice that specific figures are used in the rationale to justify the objective. This is a good idea whenever possible. A worksheet for writing objectives and a rationale is presented in Exhibit 26.

Exhibit 23
Criteria for a Good Objective

1. Relates directly to a strategic thrust.
2. Relates to mission of the organization.
3. Is clear, concise, and understandable.
4. Is stated in output or results terms.
5. Begins with "to" and an action verb. (Examples: to reduce, to increase, to implement, to meet, to develop, to replace, etc.)
6. Specifies a date for accomplishment.
7. Deals with one major subject or outcome.
8. Ties in with upper- and lower-level objectives.
9. Ties in with lateral objectives.
10. Is quantifiable.

Exhibit 24
Worksheet for Quantifying Hard to Quantify Objectives

Initial Objective: To improve our organization's image in the community by January 30, 1986.

The above objective, while admirable, is difficult to measure.

Ask These Questions:
1. How do we know we need the objective? What tells us we now have a poor community image?

2. How will we know when we have accomplished the objective? What output or performance indicators will tell us we have a better image in the community?

3. Do we now track or measure any of the above indicators?

4. If not, how difficult would it be to start tracking them?

5. Would the use of a special study (in-house or outside consultant) help us to determine some measures?

6. Are there some substitute measures we could use? (Examples: negative press or other media reports, reports from the prospective job applicants, employee turnover rates, etc.)

7. What specific factors contribute to a good image? (Examples: location of facility, general appearance of facility and vehicles, receptionist behavior, telephone manners, behavior of sales personnel, reputation of products/services, etc.)

   Possible Related Objective: To reduce the number of unfavorable press and media reports by 75 percent by January 30, 1986.

   Alternative Restated Objective: To remodel office facility and implement comprehensive landscaping program by January 30, 1986.

   Note: The specific re-stated objective would depend on the answers to the above questions.

Exhibit 25
Sample Objectives and Strategic Thrusts

MAJOR AIRLINE

Strategic Thrust: Develop innovative techniques, methods, and programs to create a whole new airline as perceived by our customers, employees, press, and stockholders in order to survive in a deregulated environment.

Objectives:

1. To institute an employee stock ownership program and have 100 percent employee participation by January 1, 1986.

2. To expand routes by instituting a Kansas City hub for East-West travel and to become the number one airline to South America by January 1, 1986.

3. To match aircraft better with route requirements in terms of load factor, fuel efficiency, distance, etc., always at a competitive fare.

4. To increase participation in the frequent flyer program by 50 percent by improving participation with other carriers, making the payoffs more desirable, and instituting a senior citizens program by July 31, 1986.

5. To maintain quality services, equipment, and a reservation system equal to, if not exceeding, pre-deregulation at fares competitive with the industry (ongoing).

DIVERSIFIED CONTAINER FIRM

Strategic Thrust: To make a strong commitment to improve earnings throughout all product lines by the end of 1987.

Objectives:

1. To continue closing less-profitable facilities and developing an organization that is simple in form and emphasizes decentralization and worldwide marketing throughout 1986.

2. To double our $600 million plastics business by the end of 1988.

3. To double our sales in the health care field through acquisition, operations in Southeast Asia, West Germany, Italy, and Mexico and through our 48 percent equity in Health Group, Inc., by the end of 1987.

4. To expand our business in financial services and leasing by 25 percent by creating a new profit center to broaden and diversify our participation in the industry by July 31, 1985.

90

Exhibit 25 (Continued)

5. To emphasize higher margin products in container board and corrugated boxes while maintaining high quality and low costs so as to improve earnings by 50 percent by the end of 1986.

6. To generate at least $50 million in cash in our glass contained business each year for the next three years.

MANUFACTURER OF HOME COMPUTERS

Strategic Thrust: To strengthen our overburdened manufacturing operations.

Objectives:

1. To install manufacturing and financial controls throughout all plants by the end of 1986.

2. To improve coordination and cooperation of internal units now competing with one another.

3. To fill all product orders from both mass merchandisers and smaller accounts by increasing production 25 percent by the end of 1986.

4. To bring out a new computer by June 30, 1986.

5. To increase value of inventory by 20 percent by September 1, 1986.

AIR CARRIER

Strategic Thrust: To expand operations in Birmingham to match Delta's operations in Atlanta by adding new routes and planes by concentrating primarily on peripheral routes and airports.

Objectives:

1. To acquire 35 new planes by May 1, 1986.

2. To add service to New Orleans, St. Louis, Denver, and Minneapolis by the end of 1987.

3. To maintain one of the lowest cost structures in the industry (ongoing).

4. To increase the number of phones and agents of reservation desk by 50 percent by April 1, 1986.

5. To improve on-time flights to at least 80 percent of total flights by May 1, 1985.

6. To inititate service to the West Coast by December 31, 1986.

7. To streamline baggage handling and other ground procedures in order to reduce the number of bags not properly loaded from 300 per day to 25 or less per day by May 1, 1986.

Exhibit 26
Worksheet for Writing Objectives

OBJECTIVE WRITING WORKSHEET

STRATEGIC THRUST:_____

_____

_____

OBJECTIVE:_____

_____

_____

_____

RATIONALE:_____

_____

_____

STRATEGIC THRUST:_____

_____

_____

OBJECTIVE:_____

_____

_____

_____

RATIONALE:_____

_____

_____

Criteria for a good objective:

1. Specific. Deals with one single key result to be accomplished.
2. Measurable, trackable. Can tell if it is accomplished.
3. Result centered not activity centered.
4. Short, simple, to the point, and understandable.
5. Quantified if possible. Has a number in it.
6. Time bounded. Specifies a date for accomplishment.
7. Begins with "to" and an action verb.
8. Realistic and sufficient. Neither too hard or too easy.
9. Consistent with superior, subordinate, and peer objectives.
10. Consistent with unit mission and strategic thrusts.

WHAT TYPE OF OBJECTIVES SHOULD BE SET?

As you look over the example objectives in Exhibit 25, you will note a variety of objectives listed. Some of these objectives are improvement objectives: they specify how the organization plans to improve some aspect of their operations. This is the most common form of objective. However, some of the objectives are equilibrium objectives. These objectives reflect the fact that the organization is satisfied with some aspect of their operations and intends to continue at the same level. Sometimes, it is wise to write equilibrium objectives if the organization is particularly proud of something it is doing or is in the middle of a major project that it wishes to keep visible until it is completed.

Notice also that the time frame on the objective varies. Even though operational objectives tend to be short range, it is not necessary that they be less than one year in length. Rather, convenient cutoff points should be used. For example, if a particular phase for a strategic thrust ends after two years, then this time frame could be used as the ending date for an operational objective. If, on the other hand, a major phase ends after two months, then this date for accomplishment could be used. There is nothing magical about the one-year period for an operational objective.

Sometimes a career development objective or two will be stated as an operational objective. Although none are shown in Exhibit 25, they are sometimes stated when the organization wishes to emphasize strongly some career development area it believes is in need of improving. For example, consider this example from the manufacturer of metal products:

Objective: To ensure that all top and middle managers are computer literate, at least with the personal computer, by the end of 1985.

Presumably, as a result of this objective, the company will develop and schedule seminars and workshops on using the small computer. They will also make personal computers available for their managers for practice.

Objectives should also deal with various organizational units. For example, if the company is organized along functional lines, then objectives should be specified for each of the major functions in the operation: manufacturing, distribution, advertising, sales, finance, personnel, accounting, marketing, and so on. If the company is organized by product group, then the objectives should be organized around product lines: consumer, industrial, international, and so on. If the organization is by geographic region, then the objectives should reflect this: Northeast, Southeast, Midwest, and so on. If customer group is the basis for organization, then the objectives should be organized along these lines; for example: residential accounts, government accounts, university accounts, military accounts, and so on. The major caution here is that top-level planners should not get involved with writing the details of the objectives for each area; rather, they should recognize that specific objectives will need to be written in each area by the managers responsible for the respective area. Of course, these specific objectives must be consistent with the strategic thrusts and overall objectives written by the top management planning group.

HOW CAN WE PRIORITIZE OBJECTIVES?

This is a sticky question that plagues many organizations. There often seems so much to do and so little time to do it. However, there are a number of actions that can be taken to prioritize the objectives. This prioritization should occur because many organizations have a tendency to focus on too many objectives at one time. This tends to dissipate energy and resources and few objectives get accomplished. We do a mediocre job trying to achieve a lot when we would have been better off doing a great job on just a few objectives.

Relate to Key Problems and Opportunities. Our environmental assessment and forecast, as well as our internal assessment, should result in some determination of priority. We want to write strategic thrusts that capitalize on the most significant environmental opportunities and overcome our most critical problems. If we keep this in mind as we write our strategic thrusts and operational objectives, we will be well on our way to establishing a priority of objectives.

Relate to Mission. Our most important strategic thrusts and objectives also should be those that are most critical to the attainment of our mission. We can determine this by placing our strategic thrusts and objectives into one of three categories as follows:

- *Must do.* These are strategic thrusts and objectives that are absolutely critical for mission attainment. If we fail in these, we fail in our mission as an organization. They are so important they cannot be postponed.
- *Ought to do.* These are also important and relate directly to our mission, but, if we fail to achieve them, it will not result in failure to achieve our mission. We may be able to temporarily postpone their achievement to a later period.
- *Nice to do.* These are also important and relate directly to our mission, (no thrust or objective should be developed that is not important) but they can be postponed for even a longer period if need be. We must eventually achieve them, however, to ensure our long-term survival.

Thus, time becomes an important criterion to determine must do, ought to do, and nice to do categories. We must be careful, however, to avoid continual postponement of ought to do and nice to do objectives or we will never achieve them. Usually, as time goes by, the nice to do becomes ought to do and the ought to do becomes must do. The length of time, however, will vary by objective.

For example, we may initially list automation of our assembly process as a nice to do objective. However, if our competitors automate and significantly reduce costs, then this objective should immediately become a must do if we expect to remain competitive.

Rank Ordering. The above method results in placing objectives within one of three categories, not a rank ordering of all thrusts and objectives. If we desire a specific rank ordering of objectives, then we need to go one step further. One good method to do this is to use the NGT and Delphi methods we have previously discussed. Another method, however, is paired comparison. Exhibit 27 shows a worksheet for this method. Here's how it works.

Exhibit 27
Worksheet to Set Priorities Using Paired Comparison Technique

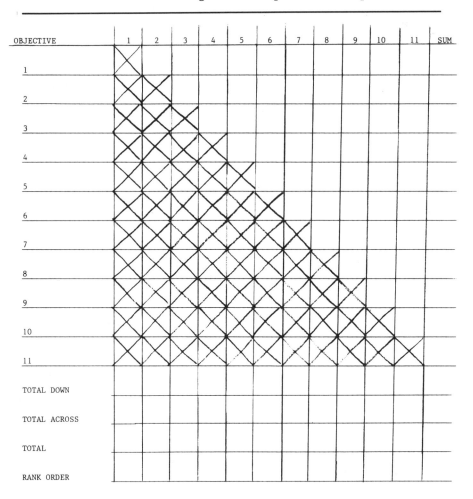

1. The objectives are numbered in a random order (not by priority) and arrayed across the top of a page and down the left-hand margin. A grid is then drawn.

2. Each decision maker or planner evaluates each objective against each other. If the objective on the left-hand side is more important than the one at the top, then a 1 is placed in the block. If it is not more important a 0 is placed in the block.

3. The horizontal and vertical total for each objective is summed.

4. The objectives are ranked in terms of their number, highest to lowest.

5. The average ranking of each objective is determined by adding all of the rankings for each objective and dividing by the number of people doing the ranking. This gives the cumulative judgment of the group as to the rank order of objectives.

The paired comparison method forces a group to determine a priority by requiring them to compare each objective to each other objective. This can be done with all objectives or only the objectives listed for each strategic thrust. After the ranking is determined, a general discussion should be held regarding the final priority.

The development and communication of operational objectives is critical if the strategic plan is to be implemented. Also critical is the development of action steps and a time frame or schedule for their accomplishment. That is the subject of the next chapter.

11.

Developing Action Steps and Schedules

This phase of the strategic planning process is concerned with determining the specific steps and timetable required for the accomplishment of each objective. It deals with the "how" and "when" of the process. Sometimes this phase is called "action planning," "programming," or "implementing." Whatever the label, it refers to the determination of the major chunks of activities that must be accomplished in order to achieve the objective and with the scheduling of these activities.

HOW ARE ACTION STEPS DEVELOPED?

The top-level strategic planning group should not formulate the specific action steps for the operational objectives unless they are actually directly responsible for the accomplishment of the objectives. The general rule to follow here is that the people expected to carry out the objective should be primarily responsible for determining the action steps. Superiors above may wish to review the action steps to ensure consistency and conformity with policy, but they should avoid the temptation of actually writing them. The determination of the action steps by the people responsible for objective accomplishment enhances participation and commitment in the strategic planning process.

When determining action steps, the major chunks of activities that need to be accomplished should be focused on. There is no need to delve into extreme detail in order to determine all the substeps involved. These substeps are important, but they need not be actually determined in the planning sessions. If the person who is going to carry out the action steps is unfamiliar with the steps to be accomplished, he or she could ask for some guidance as to the specifics under each major step. Otherwise, it is best to assume that the person who will carry out the action step knows what to do and will ask for guidance if needed.

The basic question to be asked in determining action steps is: How will we accomplish the objective? In other words, what must be done to ensure successful accomplishment of the objective? In answering this question, we need to be sure we do not leave out a major task that will need to be completed. We also need to be sure that we obtain the cooperation of any other units in the organization that will have some responsibility in helping us to complete an action step. Finally, we need to be concerned with the problem of sequence and concurrency of steps. Let's look at each of these issues.

After we write the action steps for an objective, we ought to be able to review them and say with a high degree of confidence, "Yes, if we accomplish all of the action steps we will, in fact, accomplish the objective." If we cannot say this, then it is usually because of one of two reasons: either we do not know enough to know what needs to be accomplished because the objective is new to us, or we know what needs to be done but we are not sure we can actually pull it off.

In the first case, we may not be able to achieve completeness. We may be able to determine action steps up to a certain point and then stop. For example, consider the action steps for this objective:

Objective: To reduce employee turnover from 50 percent per year to 25 percent per year by the end of 1986.

Now we suppose we have some idea of what is causing our turnover, but we are not entirely sure of all of the factors involved. We may be able to specify action steps up to a point and then set up some alternatives after that point. For example, for the above objective, we may have the following action steps:

1. To increase wage rates 10 percent to make them competitive with the local labor market.

2. To improve selection procedures to screen out better those likely to leave employment after a short period.

3. To improve working conditions in the dip room where temperatures are high and ventilation is low.

4. To implement an exit interview program to determine why people are leaving.

5. To hire a consultant to determine if supervisory practices are contributing to high turnover.

At this point, it may not be possible to specify any additional action steps until the information for steps four and five are determined. After that information is obtained, then additional action steps can be formulated.

There is another course of action that can be taken at this point, however. That step is the formulation of contingency plans. Contingency plans are used when we are not sure of the factors that will influence the course of action we should take. They are "what if" or alternative plans. We formulate contingency plans so that we are prepared for possible eventualities. Of course, we can not prepare for all likely future events; so we formulate contingency plans for the most likely occurrences. This is why probability analysis is so often used in contingency planning.

Using contingency planning in the above turnover example, we may have some idea as to the information that will likely be uncovered in steps four and five. For example, we might hypothesize that exit interviews and a review by an outside consultant will tell us that we have harsh and rather autocratic supervisory practices that are contributing to our turnover. Therefore, we could set up a contingency plan for a supervisory training program in human relations and communications in order to correct this. We might also have to set up a plan to change our recruitment and selection practices of supervisors.

On the other hand, suppose that we find that the main reason that people are leaving is because they find the work very boring and do not see an opportunity to grow. If this is the case, we may wish to plan for a job enrichment and career development program. If we suspect that this will be the case, a contingency plan along these lines would be appropriate.

In developing contingency plans, we should be careful to not overplan. That is, we cannot possibly plan for all contingencies. As we mentioned earlier, we should plan for those most likely to happen. For these, we might wish to go into some considerable detail in our plan. For those contingencies that are less likely to happen, we may only want to sketch out the briefest of plans. At least we recognize a possible eventuality, but we are not going to spend much time planning for it unless the possibility of it happening increases.

For the above turnover example, we might formulate two contingency plans as follows:

If harsh and autocratic supervisory practices are found:

Action Plan A:

6. Develop a three-day workshop for selected supervisors on human relations and communications.

7. Schedule a staff meeting to review proper supervisory practices.

8. Provide reading material on human relations and communications for supervisors.

9. Monitor supervisory performance in this area.

10. Transfer or terminate supervisors who cannot improve their performance.

If, on the other hand, boring and unchallenging jobs with low opportunity for growth is found:

Action Plan B:

6. Review job descriptions and observe job performance in jobs most often identified as boring.
7. Determine feasibility of job redesign (cost, time, new machinery, etc.).
8. Select a few jobs for a re-design effort on a pilot basis.
9. Monitor, review, and evaluate the success of this program to determine if project can be expanded.
10. During the above steps, investigate the possibility of establishing a career advancement program for employees.
11. Review present promotion procedures and paths to enhance promotion opportunities.
12. Review promote from within versus hiring on the outside policy to see if modification is needed.

Sometimes, when we do contingency planning, we run up against a whole series of questions for which we do not know the answer. We can use decision tree analysis to help us here. Exhibit 28 shows an example of a decision tree for our turnover example. Notice that the information we determine at various stages set the next stage in motion. We reach decision points when the course of action we will take will need to be decided. Decision trees are helpful when there are several unknowns and decision points in our analysis. They reflect a number of contingency plans that are specified for an objective. When a complicated decision tree is developed, we are engaging in scenario building, which we discussed earlier in the book. We lay out a series of "what if" scenarios that we then plan for.

By using contingency planning, decision trees, and scenario building, we are trying to achieve completeness in the planning process. We must also be concerned with the concurrency issue. Which steps must be done before others and which ones can be done concurrently? This is very important in planning. Think of building a house: one would not do the plumbing and wiring after the dry wall has been put up. Yet one could do plumbing and wiring at the same time. There is no need to delay a step if it can be done concurrently with another step.

HOW CAN ACTION STEPS BE SCHEDULED?

The general rule here is that the person expected to carry out the action steps should have some say as to when it can be accomplished. This does not mean that they should have the only say; those involved with establishing and accomplishing the objective should have the major responsibility for determining its date for accomplishment.

Exhibit 28
Sample Decision Tree

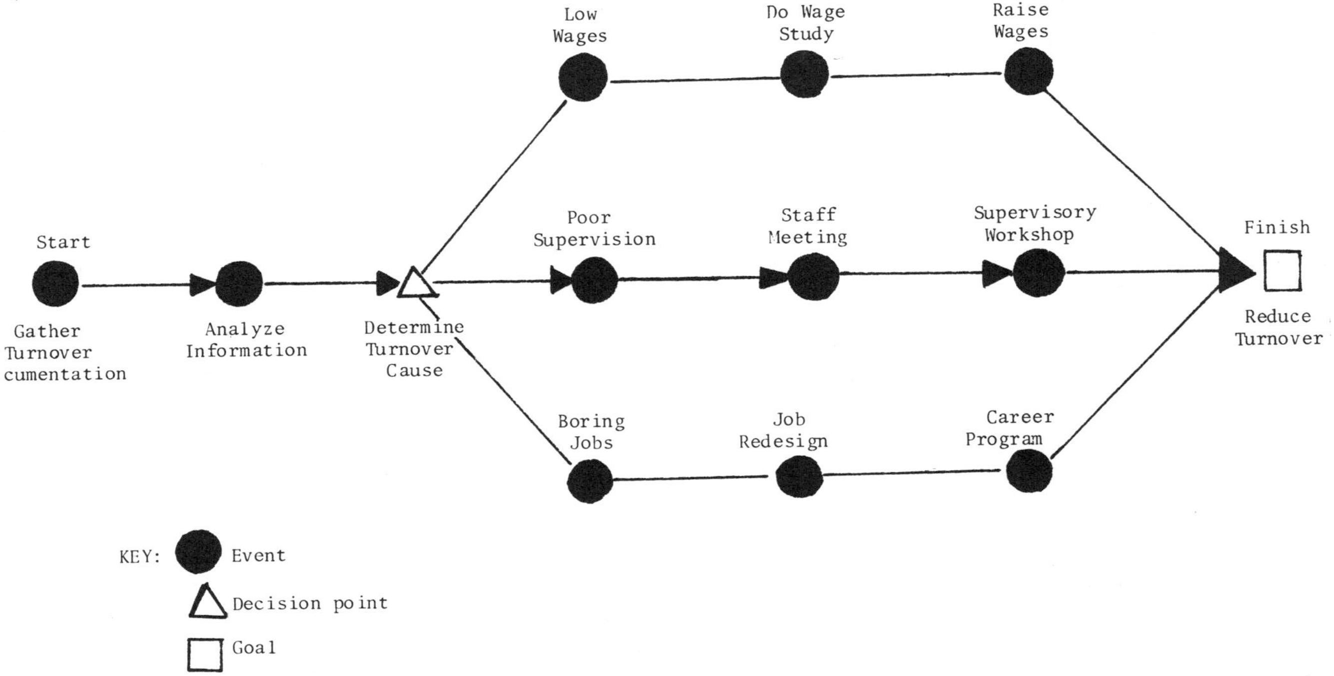

KEY:

● Event

△ Decision point

□ Goal

End-Point Scheduling

A good way to schedule is to start with the time the objective is to be accomplished and work backward to the present. For example, let's look at a simple personal situation we are all familiar with. Let's suppose it is a Saturday morning. You and your spouse decide to make dinner reservations at a local restaurant for 7:30 p.m. This was the only time open. There are a number of activities that you wish to do during the day. To ensure that you arrive for dinner on time, you decide to work backward in building a schedule. You make a list of the things you wish to do today and how long you think it will take you to do each, working backward from your dinner reservation. Let's assume that it is 9:30 a.m. and that you are having your second cup of coffee while you are doing this. The list you come up with and the time allotment looks like this:

7:30 Dinner
7:15 drive to restaurant (15 min.)
6:45 pick up babysitter (30 min.)
6:15 shower and get dressed (30 min.)
5:30 help with kids' supper (45 min.)
4:45 jog normal route (45 min.)
4:15 drive home from golf (30 min.)
12:45 play golf (3½ hrs.)
12:15 lunch at course (30 min.)
11:45 drive to course (30 min.)
11:30 get golf stuff together (15 min.)
10:30 mow grass (1 hr.)
10:00 read paper (30 min.)
 9:30 get dressed and help with dishes (30 min.)

You are going to make it! Now, most of us do not like to have our days off planned to this degree. However, this illustrates the type of scheduling that should be done to accomplish the action steps of key objectives. Incidentally, end-point scheduling can go a long way in helping us with time management both on and off the job.

In reviewing the above example, a few points become apparent. First, all steps to be accomplished should be listed. In the above example, if even one step of something we wish to do is left out of our schedule we will be late for dinner if we attempt to do it. Second, our estimated time to complete each activity should be accurate. We do not appear to have much slack in our schedule. (When do we get a chance to just relax?) Third, we need to decide how critical each event is. Can we cancel some events if we start running short of time? (We had better go ahead with the shower after such an active day.) Fourth, we need to determine if we can delegate any of the events. Perhaps we can ask the sitter to find her own transportation. Or perhaps the sitter can fix the kids their dinner if they will wait that long. Fifth, we need to determine if we can postpone the time for our dinner reservation say until 8:00 or 8:15. We also need to try to determine the penalty for being late. If we lose our reservation, how long of a wait will we have? Are there alternative restaurants close by where we could go?

The use of end-point scheduling helps us to be realistic in our scheduling because it requires that we start with the time when we wish to finish rather than the time when we can start. It is the finish time that is most important.

Realism in Scheduling

Most of us are too optimistic when we schedule. We are enthusiastic about our objective, and we think we will be able to zip right through our action steps without difficulty. We also forget that people will be sick, on vacation, or traveling—all of which can delay our schedule. Sometimes, we also do not factor in holidays, employee turnover, delays in shipment of equipment and material, and the time it sometimes takes to convince another person on whom we depend for cooperation.

For this reason, it is a good idea to schedule some slack time in our schedule. Of course, too much slack time is not good either—we think we have all the time in the world to complete the action steps when we do not. Some of us do much better in meeting objectives when we have a lot to do than when we have little to do. When we have little to do we tend to procrastinate since we know we have lots of time.

A good technique for determining realistic time frames and appropriate amounts of slack involves using optimistic-pessimistic scheduling to determine the realistic time. Exhibit 29 shows how to use this technique. First, we determine the optimistic parameter (the top line). This is determined by asking ourselves: How much time would it take to accomplish this objective if everything went well? Then we determine the pessimistic time boundary by asking ourselves: How much time would it take to accomplish this objective if everything went poorly? Finally, since we know not everything that could go wrong will go wrong and that all that could go right will not go right, we pick what we think will be the most realistic time—the middle line. This can be expressed as a range of days shown by the two dashed lines above and below the realistic time line in Exhibit 29.

The main advantage of using this technique is that it forces us to set an upper and lower boundary on our time estimates. We then focus our attention on the area within the boundary. If we are working with an unfamiliar objective or one with which we have had some trouble in the past, we will probably select an area toward the pessimistic time line as our realistic time. On the other hand, if we are working with a familiar objective that has always gone pretty smoothly in the past, we will likely choose a time near the optimistic time line as our realistic time.

WHAT ARE SOME SCHEDULING TOOLS WE CAN USE TO HELP US SCHEDULE?

There are some tools we can use to help us set and track a schedule. Some are simpler than others. A general guideline is that we should use the simplest tool that allows us to accomplish our objective. We look at four scheduling tools in this section. They are calendars, Gantt or bar charts, PERT diagrams, and tie-in sheets or forms.

Calendars

One of the simplest yet often most effective tools for scheduling is the calendar. A desk-top calendar that depicts the entire week in some detail allows us to write in when various action steps have to be accomplished during the course of a year. These can be color coded at the top of each page in terms of criticality or difficulty. Coupled with this, a tickler file by week or month can be set up to remind us to do certain things when that time period rolls around.

Exhibit 29
Optimistic-Pessimistic Scheduling to Determine Realistic Time

---

———————————————————————————— **Optimistic Time**
                                                (All goes well)

- -

———————————————————————————— **Realistic Time**
                                                (Most likely)

- -

———————————————————————————— **Pessimistic Time**
                                                (All goes poorly)

Another calendar that is handy is a pocket calendar. While not as detailed as a desk-top calendar, it has the advantage of easy portability. Certain key events can be noted on this when you are away from your desk and the information transferred to your desk calendar once you return to your office. Of course, it is important to make sure that your pocket and desk-top calendars agree with one another.

A wall calendar that depicts the entire year, week by week, month by month, is also a useful device. This allows you to see at a glance when various objectives and action steps need to be accomplished. Again, color coding makes this device even more useful.

Another helpful tool consists of a loose-leaf notebook containing both project cards and monthly calendars. On the left side of each scheduling panel is a vertical row of scheduling cards. Each project is recorded on one of these cards. Steps that need to be accomplished by whom and when are added and filed with the card in a packet. To the right is a linear scheduling calendar that provides a separate recording space for each project. Moving across the calendar, a mark or notation is placed whenever something is to happen or be checked.

The system provides a daily review of all project schedules. Locating the current date at the bottom of the calendar and moving up the column will indicate which projects need attention that day. At the same time the steps coming due in the next few days or weeks can be seen. There are several companies that publish these systems.

Gantt or Bar Charts

These were developed many years ago to help with production scheduling. A sample chart is shown in Exhibit 30 for a major consumer products manufacturer desiring to expand market share. Note that it depicts the beginning and ending dates for an event, the sequencing of events, and the extent to which an event is completed (shown by shaded line, but could be shown with color code). As the action steps are accomplished, the shaded line is drawn in. If a barrier or hurdle is reached that causes delay in achieving an action step, either a triangle or block can be drawn in. Notice in the example that we exceed our estimated time on our first two steps. Notice that we ran into an immediate barrier on our third step which caused us to delay the beginning of this step for six months. However, we were able to begin and end our fourth step as scheduled. At the present time in the example we are at April 1, 1986. A blank Gantt or bar chart for your use is provided in Exhibit 31. This chart can be used for each objective developed.

PERT Chart

A more complicated scheduling and control technique involves the use of a PERT chart. PERT stands for Program Evaluation Review Tech-

Exhibit 30
Gantt or Bar Chart for Scheduling

OBJECTIVE: To increase market share by 25 percent by June 30, 1987.

Action Steps:

1. Change theme of national ad campaign
2. Increase advertising budget by 30 percent
3. Expand distribution channels in S.E.
4. Expand production capacity by installing third shift
5. Expand warehouse space
6. Change packaging to make more eye-catching
7. Bring out reduced calorie version of product
8. Run "cents-off" coupon promotion
9. Install improved incentive system for distributors
10. Sponsor fraternity parties
11. Improve point-of-purchase display

July 1 1985	Oct.1	Jan 1 1986	Apr.1	July 1	Oct.1	Jan.1 1987	Apr.1	July 1

KEY:

completed ▨

scheduled ▮

barrier ▲

Exhibit 31
Worksheet Form for Gantt or Bar Chart for Scheduling

OBJECTIVE:

Action Steps:

1.

2.

3.

4.

5.

6.

7.

8.

9.

10.

11.

12.

(Time)

nique. It was developed in the aerospace industry during the decades of the fifties and sixties. The technique involves graphically laying out the sequence of steps or events that must be accomplished in order to achieve an objective. The time to complete each event is clearly specified. Finally, a critical path is determined. The critical path (CP) is the longest sequence between the series of events. It is considered the critical path since any delay in this path will delay the entire project. That is, we can experience a delay in any other sequence of events without delaying the entire project. Of course, if the delay in another sequence of events is of such a magnitude that the sequence of events involved becomes the longest path, then we will have established a new critical path. Since it is difficult to focus our attention on all events in a project, the critical path allows us to focus on the most critical series of events that must be accomplished on time to ensure that the objective is reached on time.

Let's look at an example. Exhibit 32 presents a simple version of a PERT diagram for merging two organizational divisions. Note that this PERT diagram is simplified for discussion purposes. An actual diagram for such an event would be much more complicated than depicted here.

We begin at the left-hand side of the figure where a decision has been made to merge the two organizational units. Someone has been assigned the authority to plan and carry through with the merger. Then we lay out all the key steps that must be accomplished in order to complete the merger. (Normally, only the dots are shown, but for purposes of our discussion, the actual step is spelled out.) Next we write in the realistic number of days it will actually take to accomplish each event. Then we compute the longest series of days between events: this is our critical path.

As we progress through the sequence of steps, we can use the diagram to track our performance. We might color code our progress—green for completion on time, yellow for possible days, and red for delays and blockages. As we go through the project, we may need to add or delete steps and change our time estimates. However, even though every planning tool or document needs to be flexible, we need to be careful that we do not continually change the document so that it becomes meaningless.

Each of the major steps in Exhibit 30 will likely have a PERT chart of its own that depicts the substeps involved in each major step. These can be attached to the major PERT diagram or can simply be left with the people responsible for accomplishing them.

Tie-in Sheets

As you can see by now, it is easy to get lost in a sea of paperwork. However, there are some things we can do to minimize the paperwork overload. First, any time we can load our information onto a computer, we should do so. The new microcomputers are handy for this task. Second, any time we can use data already being collected, we should do

Exhibit 32
Simplified PERT Diagram of Merger between Two Organizational Units

Objective: To complete the merger of the Devcor and Ryner Divisions by August 1, 1987.

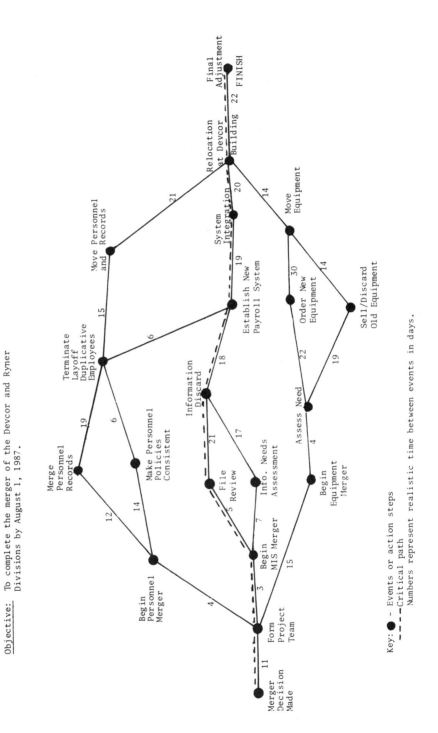

Key: ● - Events or action steps
 ----Critical path
 Numbers represent realistic time between events in days.

so. We should avoid generating new reports and data collection procedures as much as possible. Third, we should try to use tie-in sheets as
much as possible to summarize our plan. We discuss two tie-in sheets that
many people have found useful in planning.

The first sheet is found in Exhibit 33. Notice that in this one form we
specify the objective to be accomplished, the action steps, the date for

Exhibit 33
Worksheet for Tie-in of Objectives

OBJECTIVE: _____

ACTION STEPS:	Date for Completion	Person Accountable	Tracking or Measuring System
1.			
2.			
3.			
4.			
5.			

Exhibit 33 (Continued)

ACTION STEPS: 6.	Date for Completion	Person Accountable	Tracking or Measuring System
_____			
_____			
_____			
7._____			
_____			
_____			
_____			
8._____			
_____			
_____			
9._____			
_____			
_____			
10._____			
_____			
_____			

completion for each action step, the person accountable for completion, and the tracking or measuring system we will use for the action step. This simple form tells us what (objective), how (action steps), when (completion dates), and who (person accountable). It also tells us how we can track the objective in the way of a specific report, a meeting, or a chart. This column should also specify any key indicators we will use to track the objective, such as turnover rates, market share, or sales. Exhibit 34 shows a completed example.

We should have one of these tie-in sheets for each of our key objectives to be accomplished. The strategic planning group should have a notebook containing all the objectives. Each manager who is expected to help achieve the key objectives should also have a notebook of not only his or her objectives, but also those objectives with which he or she must interact or help out.

Exhibit 34
Sample Worksheet for Tie-in of Objectives

OBJECTIVE: To reduce quality control rejects by 50% by September 1, 1986.

ACTION STEPS:	Date for Completion	Person Accountable	Tracking or Measuring System
1. Introduce manual dexterity test in selection procedure	12/15/85	Jorgenson, Training & Development	Quarterly training report
2. Improve component parts inspection	11/1/85	Rather, Q.C.	Weekly Q.C. report
3. Add override training element to OJT program	12/15/85	Klien, production	Weekly prod. staff meeting
4. Add one expediter/trouble shooter to each shift	1/15/86	Pankowski, personnel	Monthly personnel report
5. Introduce repo inspection at second stage of assembly	2/15/86	Ragmelli Production	Weekly prod. staff meeting

The second type of tie-in sheet is found in Exhibit 35. This sheet lays out the key objectives for the planning period and the key action steps for each objective. What really enhances the usefulness of the sheet is that all the key objectives and action steps are summarized on one sheet of paper. To facilitate this, codes or key words can be used rather than spelling out each objective or action step. This information can be transferred to a large wall chart and color coded. Using erasable markings

Exhibit 34 (Continued)

ACTION STEPS: 6.	Date for Completion	Person Accountable	Tracking or Measuring System
Convert roto track to VMF made	4/15/86	Gomez Production	Weekly Production staff meeting
7. Phase out linear joiner and replace with circle slip	7/15/86	Smith Engineering	Monthly Engineering report
8. Change specifications for lateral transverse arm to higher tolerances	8/15/86	O'Mally Engineering	Monthly Engineering report
9.			
10.			

allows one to make revisions without re-doing the whole chart. An example of this tie-in sheet is shown in Exhibit 36.

WHAT ARE SOME KEY TIME MANAGEMENT ISSUES IN SCHEDULING?

Many executives and managers today are increasingly concerned with improving their time management ability. While a complete discussion of this topic is beyond the scope of this book, we do review some key ideas on time management, particularly as they relate to the strategic planning process. The bibliography at the end of the book lists some additional references for those wishing more detailed information on time management.

Exhibit 35
Worksheet for Tying in Objectives with Key Action Steps

OBJECTIVE	KEY ACTION STEPS
1.	
2.	
3.	
4.	
5.	
6.	
7.	
8.	
9.	
10.	
11.	
12.	
13.	
14.	
15.	

TIME LINE
(in days, weeks, or months)

Exhibit 36

Sample Worksheet for Tying in Objectives with Action Steps

OBJECTIVES	KEY ACTION STEPS
1. Reduce Q.C. rejects by 25 percent	roto assembly ac. check | change selection test | cross training program | add expiditer | ▽ deadline
2. Reduce employee turnover by 20 percent	change selection method | complete wage survey | increase wages | institute employee service program | ▽ deadline
3. Expand western salesforce by 50 percent	complete sales force analysis | hire new sales people | ▽ deadline
4. Open Dallas facility	complete construction | install equipment | move employees | ▽ deadline
5. Achieve MIS implementation	complete systems analysis | order equipment | install test equip-ment | ▽ deadline
6. Remodel home offices	develop specifications | decide on bids | begin remodeling | ▽ deadline
7. Expand N.E. District Network	initiate contract program | complete contract program | expand present dist. | ▽ deadline
8. Introduce turo product	complete mrt.reg. | complete R&D | ▽ test market
9. Set in place employee port. prog.	train super. | complete quality circle | tie to incentive system | ▽ deadline
10. Expand advertising budget	reallocate budget | select ad agencies | change ad theme | ▽ deadline
11. Revise policy Manual	assign board study | report of board study | review and revise | ▽ deadline
12.	
13.	
14.	
15.	

TIME LINE (months): Mar. 1 Apr. 1 May 1 Jun. 1 Jul. 1 Aug. 1 Sept. 1 Oct. 1 Nov. 1 Dec. 1 Jan. 1 Feb. 1 Mar. 1 Apr. 1 May 1 Jun. 1 Jul. 1 Aug. 1

Time as a Resource

Most of us view time as a constraint, not as a resource. There is never enough time to do what we want to do. There is a fine but important line between viewing time as a resource versus viewing it as a constraint. When viewed as a resource, we see it as a precious commodity to be allocated and accounted for as for any precious commodity. We realize that there will never be enough time. The issue becomes one of allocating the time we have in the most effective and efficient manner possible. We should be just as concerned as to how we spend our time as we are as to how we spend our money. When we approach time management from this perspective, time management problems become resource allocation problems. As the old saying goes, "Time is money."

In allocating any resource, we are concerned with the costs versus the benefits compared with the costs and benefits of other alternatives. When we make a dollar investment, we compare our potential return with our dollar cost and the risk involved. This comparison is made with other ways we could invest our money. The same type of comparison should be made with regard to how we spend our time. How much return are we getting on a given investment of time relative to other ways we could spend our time? The greatest cost in spending our time is the opportunity cost—the foregone way we could have spent our time.

Thus, the first step to good time management is to know priorities. If the strategic planning process has been done properly, this should not be a problem; everyone should be aware of the priorities. These priorities are what the organization has agreed to as being the highest return items. Spending our time working toward these priorities is better than spending our time working toward something else.

Time Log

The second step to good time management is to know how we now spend our time. This involves keeping a time log. Exhibit 37 presents a sample time log that can be completed for a number of days (usually three to five) to determine how you now spend your time. The columns allow you to make some evaluative judgments on the quality of your time expenditure.

Once you complete the time log, ask yourself the questions shown in Exhibit 38. They may not be easy to answer and you may be surprised at some of the answers.

If you are like most people, chances are you will identify a number of time wasters. A summary of the more common time wasters is presented in Exhibit 39.

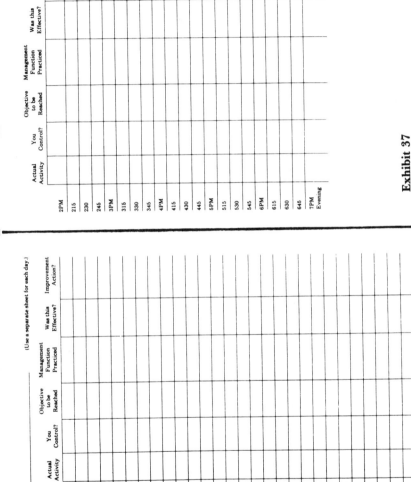

Date: _____ (Use a separate sheet for each day.)

	Actual Activity	You Control?	Objective to be Reached	Management Function Practiced	Was this Effective?	Improvement Action?
7AM						
715						
730						
745						
8AM						
815						
830						
845						
9AM						
915						
930						
945						
10AM						
1015						
1030						
1045						
11AM						
1115						
1130						
1145						
12N						
1215						
1230						
1245						
1PM						
115						
130						
145						

	Actual Activity	You Control?	Objective to be Reached	Management Function Practiced	Was this Effective?	Improvement Action?
2PM						
215						
230						
245						
3PM						
315						
330						
345						
4PM						
415						
430						
445						
5PM						
515						
530						
545						
6PM						
615						
630						
645						
7PM Evening						

Exhibit 37
Time Log and Evaluation Sheet

Exhibit 38
Analyzing Your Time Audit

- What am I doing that does not need to be done at all?
- What items am I spending too much time on?
- What items am I spending too little time on?
- What am I doing that could be done better (more economically and effectively) by others?
- Do I plan my work daily and evaluate my progress?
- Do I budget and schedule time according to priorities?
- Does my schedule allow for flexibility?
- Are some people taking too much of my time?
- Am I providing a balanced distribution of my time among my subordinates?
- Am I plagued by telephone and visitor interruptions?
- Where do I spend my time? Is it more worthwhile for me to be in one place as opposed to another?
- Do I spend a lot of time in meetings?
- Do I often get bogged down with paperwork?
- Are my written and/or verbal communications contributing to time problems?
- Do time slippage patterns surface in my audit? In what ways does time slip in the same way every day?
- Do I have time to think?

Exhibit 39
Leading Time Wasters

1. Telephone interruptions
2. Visitors dropping in without appointments
3. Meetings, both scheduled and unscheduled
4. Crisis situations for which no plans were possible
5. Lack of objectives, priorities, and deadlines
6. Cluttered desk and personal disorganization
7. Involvement in routine and detail that should be delegated to others
8. Attempting too much at once and underestimating the time it takes to do it
9. Failure to set up clear lines of responsibility and authority
10. Inadequate, inaccurate, or delayed information from others
11. Indecision and procrastination
12. Lack of or unclear communication and instruction
13. Inability to say "no"
14. Lack of standards and progress reports that enable a company manager to keep track of developments
15. Fatigue

Source: "How to Make the Most of Your Time." *U.S. World News and World Report*, December 3, 1973, pp. 45–54.

Exhibit 40
Managing Telephone Calls

• Incoming Calls

    Have secretary give name when answering

    Keep secretary informed of important information: new contacts and the names of their secretaries

    Have secretary screen, establish purpose, and re-direct when appropriate

    Establish call-back system

    Refer selected call-backs to secretary

• Outgoing calls

    Call-back when contact is likely

    Group related calls

    Have information convenient for quick retrieval

    Have subject outlined

    Leave complete message with secretary when no direct contact is made

• Get to the Point of the Conversation and Maintain Control

• Avoid Being a Holder or a Holdee

• Curtail Your Calls by Weighing Your Words

    Be honest and candid in terminating your conversation after satisfying the purpose

    Do not invite people to call back sometime

• Utilize the Conference Call

• Utilize a Hideaway

• Utilize an Answering Device

• Utilize an Egg Timer

• Utilize a Progressive Buzzer

• Limit Personal Calls

Manage Interruptions

Usually, a time log reveals that there are quite a few interruptions that cause us to not spend our time in the most efficient manner possible. Interruptions cause inefficiency because we have to stop what we are doing, take care of the interruption, and then re-focus our thoughts before we can start up with what we were doing to begin with. Some people are better than others in doing this, but for all of us interruptions are still time wasters.

Exhibit 41
Managing Office Visits

- Schedule regular formal and informal meetings.
- Establish appointment hours.
- Operate with a modified closed-door policy.
- Authorize secretary to screen and to schedule appointments.
- Post a notice at your secretary's desk that you have asked her to screen all visitors.
- Time limit on the visit: specify time for ending a conference before you begin and inform of your next task.
- Have secretary monitor visits by phoning in.
- Meet at a location other than your office.
- Go out to meet your drop-in visitors or greet the individual at your door.
- Schedule a later meeting time.
- Confer standing up.
- Give the visitor a task to perform.
- Walk your guest to the door and be candid in explaining that you are due for your next task.
- Schedule social appointments.
- Check your furniture design for the comfort index.
- Place a refrain-from-smoking sign on your desk.
- Establish a quiet hour policy in your office.
- Utilize a hideaway.
- Be honest.

The two most common interruptions are the telephone and unannounced office visitors. Exhibits 40 and 41 present some ideas we can use to help reduce interruptions caused by the telephone and visitors.

Manage Meetings

Meetings are essential for almost every organization, but they can be great time wasters. Here's some simple guidelines to keep in mind to make meetings more efficient.

Exhibit 42
Twenty Questions for Delegation

yes	no		
___	___	1.	Do you take work home too regularly?
___	___	2.	Do you work longer hours than your subordinates?
___	___	3.	Do you spend time doing for others what they could be doing for themselves?
___	___	4.	When you return from an absence from your office, do you find your in-basket too full?
___	___	5.	Are you still handling activities and problems you had before your last promotion?
___	___	6.	Are you often interrupted with queries or requests on ongoing projects and assignments?
___	___	7.	Do you spend time on routine details that others could handle?
___	___	8.	Do you like to keep a finger in every pie?
___	___	9.	Do you keep most of the coordinating responsibilities?
___	___	10.	Do you find yourself trying to do too many different things at the same time?
___	___	11.	Do you delegate mainly the unpleasant tasks?
___	___	12.	Do you tend to delegate specific activities while retaining tight control?
___	___	13.	Do you specify due dates when you delegate?
___	___	14.	Is there an organizational incentive for you to delegate and develop your people?
___	___	15.	Have you developed the habit of delegating before doing?
___	___	16.	Do you make use of delegation files?
___	___	17.	Do you delegate more than one task at a time?
___	___	18.	Have you established a working development and delegation plan for your subordinates?
___	___	19.	Do you motivate when you delegate?
___	___	20.	Do you think you can delegate more and more effectively?

Source: Time Life & Lee, Box 398, Crawfordville, Fla.

- Be sure the meeting is really necessary before calling it. Have the objective of the meeting clearly established and determine whether a meeting is really necessary to accomplish the objective.
- Develop and distribute an agenda and any supporting documents to be discussed at the meeting enough in advance so they can be studied. Be sure people invited to the meeting really need to be there.
- Choose a convenient time. Avoid early morning and late afternoons. Avoid meetings outside of normal working hours, if possible. Try to keep normal meetings to an hour or two at most. Start and end on time.
- Encourage discussion but keep it on track. Use the agenda as a guide. Do not let one or two people dominate the discussion. Try to find out any hidden agendas people have brought with them that are subverting the purpose of the meeting.
- Try to conclude the meeting by agreeing who will do what by when.
- Keep and distribute accurate minutes of the meeting.
- Evaluate every meeting. Was it necessary? Did it accomplish the objective? Did it start and stop on time? Was the discussion fruitful and on target? What needs to be done next?

Delegate

Finally, good time management usually means more delegation. We should not do our subordinates' work for them. We should not feel that something will not get done right unless we do it ourselves. We need to develop our subordinates so that they are responsible and will willingly accept the delegation of authority and duties we give to them. We need to be quite clear as to these delegations as to what is to be done by what date. Delegation should focus on making our subordinates accountable for performance. If we do this, we can manage by exception, by getting involved when our subordinates have problems or seek our advice, rather than watching over their shoulders constantly. The quiz in Exhibit 42 can help you do a better job of delegating.

Following these time management guidelines will help keep the scheduled on track. Now we turn to budgeting, the next step in the strategic planning process.

12.

Tying to the Budget

We pointed out in Chapter 1 that one key difference between normal planning and strategic planning is that strategic planning requires a substantial commitment of resources. Unless these resources are forthcoming, the plan is nothing but a paper exercise— it will not be implemented. Since most resources in the organization are expressed in terms of financial expenditure, the plan ultimately must be tied to the budget.

For an organization just starting out with strategic planning, this tie-in with the budget might not be possible the first year or two of planning. This is okay, but at some point, the tie-in with the budget should occur. Because of the necessity of this tie-in, the planning cycle should become consistent with the budgeting cycle.

WHY BUDGET?

Everything we do in an organization costs us something. This cost can be financial or it can be in the form of effort, time, space, psychology, or opportunity. When we budget, we explicitly recognize these costs as they relate to specific objectives and we make a judgment as to whether the benefits derived from the objective are worth the costs. Since we have a limited number of resources—financial, effort, etc.—we want to spend our resources where we can get the greatest return. We can compare the costs and anticipated returns of various objectives and then focus on those that will give us the greatest return for our expenditures. It is for this reason that our plan should be most flexible at this stage. After we "price out" our objectives we may wish to modify, add, or delete objectives from our list. Until we actually put our objectives in dollars-and-cents terms, it is easy to be just "pie in the sky" with our objectives. They sound good on paper, but they are just too expensive and impractical to obtain. The budgeting process forces us to be realistic.

When we budget, we are not suggesting that we hold off on a worth-while objective just because we do not have the money for it right now. We might be able to get the money. Budgeting involves not only allocating present resources, but also future resources that are reasonable and attainable at a reasonable cost.

WHAT ARE SOME WAYS TO BUDGET?

A complete discussion of various budgeting methods is beyond the scope of this book. Rather, we briefly outline two basic approaches of budgeting and present a recommendation that has been tested in numerous workshops.

Incremental Budgeting

This is "add-on" budgeting. The budget for the previous fiscal year is taken as is and a new portion or increment is added to it for the coming fiscal year. This is a very common method of budgeting. The major advantage is its simplicity. We do not have to build an entire budget; we are only concerned with the new funding required.

The increment can be computed several ways. We can simply add an inflation factor to last year's budget. Or we can simply total the cost of new objectives we wish to accomplish this year and add this figure to last year's budget. Or we can total the cost of all modifications we make to last year's objectives and add these to last year's figure. Of course, we can use a combination of these approaches.

The primary disadvantage to incremental budgeting is that we accept last year's figure as a given. Consequently, we do not review whether the money spent last year should be spent this year. We do not thoroughly review what we have been doing and question whether we should keep doing it. We do not thoroughly examine whether the funds could be better spent on alternative objectives.

Another problem with incremental budgeting is budget integrity. We might ask for more money than we really need because we know our request will be cut. And, in fact, our request is cut because the people who allocate the money suspect that we have asked for more than we need. It becomes a vicious circle that is hard to break. The budgeting process becomes a game of one party trying to outwit the other party.

Zero-Based Budgeting

Because of these problems, an alternative budgeting technique was developed during the seventies that requires the budget to be built from the ground up or "zero." This method is also called Program Planning

Budgeting Systems (PPBS). This is a more complicated method that requires planners to build the budget around the objectives to be accomplished. Philosophically, it is more in tune with the type of budgeting we envision in the strategic planning model we discuss in this book. Note that the budgeting process does not formally enter our strategic planning process until we have decided what we want to do (objectives), how we are going to do it (action steps), and when we plan to do it (schedule). In other words, our budget is not decided until we have done our planning.

This method allows us to justify our budget better. It also helps us to set priorities. If our budget request is cut, we can be quite specific as to the specific objectives that will be affected. Some objectives will need to be eliminated or postponed. Others will need to be modified. If we receive additional monies, we can be quite specific as to what we can do to achieve additional objectives.

The greatest problem with this type of budgeting is its complicated nature. The Carter Administration used this technique, and it was not uncommon for accompanying "decision packages" for the budget to reach several volumes. Because of the added paperwork and complications, many organizations abandoned this approach.

However, the approach can be simplified by using the form suggested in Exhibit 43. Note that this form states the objective, action steps, and the schedule and cost of each action step. Totaling the cost of each action

Exhibit 43
Worksheet for Building Budget Around Objectives

OBJECTIVE: _____
_____
_____

ACTION STEPS: Completion   Person   Tracking   Cost
                          Date   Account.

1. _____
2. _____
3. _____
4. _____
5. _____
6. _____
7. _____
8. _____
9. _____
10. _____

                              Total Cost

step gives us the cost of achieving the objective. Totaling the cost of all of our objectives for a given period gives us our budget for the period.

Let's look at an example. Exhibit 44 presents a budget for an objective of reducing quality control rejects, which we discussed earlier in the

Exhibit 44
Sample Budgeting Tie-in Sheet

OBJECTIVE: To reduce quality control rejects by 50 percent by September 1, 1986

Action Steps	Completion Date	Person Accountable	Tracking	Cost
1. Introduce manual dexterity test in selection procedure	10/15/85	Jorgenson	Training department	$1,500
2. Improve components inspection	11/1/85	Rather	Q C. 500 report	
3. Add override training element to OJT program	12/15/85	Klien	Production staff meeting	750
4. Add one expediter/ troubleshooter to each shift	1/15/86	Pankowski	Personnel report	45,000
5. Introduce repo inspection at second stage of assembly	2/15/86	Ragmelli	Production staff meeting	350
6. Convert roto track to VMF mode	4/15/86	Gomez	Production staff meeting	500
7. Phase out linear joiner and replace with circle slip	7/15/86	Smith	Engineering report	3,500
8. Change specifications for lateral transverse arm to higher tolerances	8/15/86	O'Malley	Engineering report	6,500
			TOTAL:	$58,600

book. Notice that we have estimated a cost to achieve each of the action steps and that the total of these costs gives us the cost of achieving the objective. We develop the cost for each action step based on our previous experience and judgment. Of course, if we are faced with an entirely new objective, we will need to do some research before we are able to make any estimates. The more unfamiliar the objective, the more likely our estimated budget will be in error. Yet this should not deter us from making the best estimate that we can make.

I've used this approach in workshops and in consulting and find that it works. The estimates may need to be revised several times before the participants feel comfortable with the figures, but the collective judgment and background research usually result in budget figures that are pretty accurate. Of course, flexibility is as necessary in this stage of the planning process as it is in all other stages. Just because a dollar figure is committed to paper does not mean it is not subject to negotiation and modification. The key here is with adequate forecasting and assessment. If we have done a good job anticipating the factors that will influence our planning and have done a good job of assessing where we are now, our budget figures will likely be more accurate.

When we budget, we ought to key in on the critical factors. For example, in Exhibit 44, we are spending quite a bit of money to cut quality control rejects. We need to be sure that the benefits of improving product quality are worth the high cost. Also, note in Exhibit 44 that the largest portion of our expenditure is with hiring one expeditor to each shift. Perhaps we could still reach our objective without having to hire these additional people. Or perhaps we could transfer some people. Most of the other expenditures are relatively small.

Budgets are planning and control documents. As we go through the planning period we will want to compare our actual expenditures with our budgeted amounts. This requires a tracking and measuring system. It also means that we must have some standards as a basis of comparison for measuring purposes. These ideas are the subject of the next chapter.

13.

Tracking, Measuring, and Standards

The best strategic plan is meaningless unless we have some way of monitoring and measuring how we are doing. Without this, the plan becomes nothing more than a paper exercise: Why should we be concerned with performance since we know there is no way to tell how we will do in achieving our objectives?

We have already addressed the importance of tracking when we discussed the requirements for an effective objective. At that time, we said that the objective should be measurable and verifiable. We also indicate a column on our tie-in sheet where we are quite specific as to what means will be used to track an objective. In this chapter, we review some ideas to keep in mind when setting up measuring and tracking systems.

WHAT ARE THE CHARACTERISTICS OF A GOOD TRACKING SYSTEM?

Most of us are already familiar with the requirements of a good tracking and measuring system, so the review here will be rather brief.

Timeliness. The information that we receive ought to be received on a timely basis. We ought to receive fresh information so that we can act on it if necessary before things get out of hand.

Accuracy. No system provides 100 percent accurate information all of the time. However, the system that is used should have a high degree of accuracy so that we do not need to continually verify figures or act on faulty information.

Cost Effectiveness. It ought not to cost us more to gather the information that it is worth. There should be a good reason to obtain the information and this reason should justify the cost of gathering and analyzing the information.

Computer Based. With today's generation of micro-, mini-, and mainframe computers there is no reason why a substantial portion of our information handling should not be done by computer. This enhances greatly the ease of access and update and substantially reduces the paperwork and storage space required for information. It also helps us to analyze more quickly and accurately volumes of information.

User Language. The information provided to the strategic planners and other decision makers should be in language and formats that they desire. This is very important since sometimes it is the computer experts who dictate language and format. Information needs to be user based and friendly. With today's equipment, there is no reason why this cannot be so.

Relevancy. The information that we receive ought to pertain to the strategic objectives that we are tracking. Extraneous information should be kept to a minimum so that we do not suffer from information overload caused by wading through reams of unwanted and unnecessary paper. The person who is receiving the information should have the major say in determining what is relevant.

Appropriate Medium. The information should be delivered via the appropriate medium. Sometimes, an office conversation or a phone call is all that is needed. Other times, a memo, letter, or report is necessary. Still on other occasions, a complete report with a computer printout is required. Staff meetings with appropriate visual aids are also helpful to present tracking information. Finally, on-line access to a data base stored in a computer and displayed graphically is a very convenient manner to obtain the information.

Minimal Duplication. Our information systems should not be redundant. We should develop a data base that we can use for many purposes in tracking our objectives. We ought not have to go out and create a new data base or a series of reports that duplicate what we already have someplace else in the organization.

There is one other key factor in designing a tracking and measuring system: We need to anchor it with a set of standards.

WHAT ARE STANDARDS AND HOW ARE THEY USED IN THE PLANNING PROCESS?

Standards are benchmarks of comparison. They give us a frame of reference when making evaluations of our tracking information. There are five basic types of standards: historical, like-group comparison, time, legal, and engineering. Each of these is discussed below.

Historical. This compares how we are doing to how we have done in the past. We develop some measure of past performance and use that as the basis to compare our present performance. If employee turnover had been at a 75 percent annual rate for each of the past three years and it is now at 35 percent, then we can say that there has been a substantial improvement in the turnover rate. Most of the historical standards that we develop should come from the assessment phase of the strategic planning process.

Like-Group Comparison. We ought to be concerned as to how we are performing compared to others in our industry. If our profit margin is 3 percent and the industry average is 10 percent, we have a problem. We also might want to compare ourselves to organizations in other industries, especially if we are considering diversification. Also, we may want to compare ourselves to organizations of similar size and product/service line.

Sometimes we might be in an industry that sets industry-wide standards. For example, the telecommunications industry has numerous standards of service dealing with call completion rates, operator assistance time, dial tone interval, and so on. Professional associations and accrediting associations also set standards for organizations in their industry. For example, hospitals, prisons, and schools all have accreditation standards to meet. Professional groups such as nurses, lawyers, and architects also set professional standards that must be met by members of the profession. All of these standards should be considered in developing standards to go along with the strategic plan.

Time. Time standards are also important. If we wish to decrease employee turnover by 50 percent by June 1, 1987, then we had better set monthly or quarterly standards that we hope to meet as we approach June 1, 1987. For example, if we are starting July 1, 1986, we might set quarterly standards to reduce turnover as follows:

Oct. 1, 1986	20 percent
Jan. 1, 1987	15 percent
Mar. 1, 1987	10 percent
June 1, 1987	5 percent

These quarterly reductions in the annual turnover rate reflect the fact that it will probably be easier to achieve reductions early in the program and more difficult later in the program. At the end of the period, the turnover rate will be cut by 50 percent if we meet these standards.

To the extent we can work these standards into the objective or action steps, we should do so. Our action steps might relate a specific step to the amount of turnover we think it will cut.

Legal. There are zoning codes, health codes, occupational safety and health laws, pollution control laws, EEO laws, and numerous other laws and regulations that set standards of performance and operation. For example, many organizations now have a significant list of objectives and standards in both EEO and safety and health. There are few if any areas in business that surpass these two areas as far as federal law and regulations.

Engineering. Stress tolerances, chemical composition, metallurgy, time

Exhibit 45
Tie-In Sheet for Standards

OBJECTIVE: _____
_____
_____

RATIONALE: _____
_____
_____

KEY STANDARDS:

    Past Performance· _____

    Industry: _____

    Professional: _____

    Legal: _____

    Engineering: _____

ACTION STEPS: Time Standards

1. _____

2. _____

3. _____

4. _____

5. _____

6 _____

7. _____

8, _____

9, _____

10 _____

and motion study—all of these and more specify manufacturing, construction, mining, and job design standards. These standards must be built into many objectives and action steps.

So we see that the effect of standards is that they help us compare our performance and expectations against an established set of criteria or benchmarks. This makes it easier for us to form judgments about how we are doing. Of course, we also consider standards when we originally do the assessment and write the objectives. Exhibit 45 presents an example of a form that can be used to tie in standards with objectives and action steps.

We now move to the last step of the strategic planning process. This step involves taking corrective action based on the monitoring and tracking information. It is an attempt to bring out of line performance back to desired performance.

14.

Systems for Corrective Action

As the old saying goes, "the best laid plans of mice and men. . . ." Very seldom does actual performance exactly match desired or planned performance. Consequently, every strategic plan needs a system of corrective action. This system must rely on information gathered in the tracking and monitoring phase discussed in the previous chapter. To a large extent, the quality and timeliness of this information will determine the effectiveness of the system for corrective action. Therefore, the first step in the corrective action system is to have an effective monitoring and tracking system for the plan.

WHAT ARE CORRECTIVE ACTION SYSTEMS?

Corrective action systems attempt to bring out-of-line performance back on line in accordance with the strategic plan. Usually, the system addresses one or all of the following factors: performance of people, performance of machines or equipment, or the adequacy of the goals and objectives. Let's look at each of these factors.

Performance of People

The performance of the people involved in achieving the plan may be deficient for a number of reasons:

1. The people do not know what is expected of them. We may not have been explicit as to the meaning of various objectives and action steps in the plan. We may not have communicated the plan effectively to those who must carry it out.

2. The people may not have adequate education and training to carry out their duties under the plan. They may know what they are to do but may not know how they are to do it.

3. The people may not desire to carry out objectives. Their level of motivation may be low because either they have a low level of aspiration or they do not see many incentives and rewards for meeting the plan.
4. Emergencies and crises may be so frequent that people are deterred from carrying out the plan. Poor forecasting and the development of contingency plans may cause people to lose site of the plan completely when an emergency or crisis comes about.
5. Work overload can keep people from reaching objectives if they are given more work to do under the plan on top of an already full workload.

It is essential that the planning staff anticipate and try to prevent these problems. If they do occur, it is important that action be taken to resolve them quickly before the entire plan is jeopardized. If these problems persist, people will begin to work as if there were no plan at all.

Performance of Machines or Equipment

We cannot expect people to do an outstanding job in meeting objectives under a plan if they do not have the proper equipment and tools. For example, in the later half of the decade of the seventies, exhortations to steelworkers in the United States to "work harder and faster" to meet Japanese competition were largely fruitless. The obsolete plant and equipment of our steel mills prevented viable competition with the Japanese who rely on much newer and more efficient equipment. Until steelworkers have modern plants and equipment, it will be difficult to be competitive in world markets with steel.

This situation presents itself too often today. We blame people for poor performance when it is the tools, plant, and equipment that need addition. Granted, people make decisions about plant and equipment, but these decisions are usually made at the highest levels of the organization. Top-level managers need to take the responsibility for making capital equipment decisions; the blame does not rest with workers.

Therefore, if objectives under the plan are not being reached, we need to investigate the role being played by tools, plant, and equipment. If we have done a proper internal assessment and a proper assessment of available technology in the environment prior to developing our plan, we should be better able to determine the impact that tools and equipment will have in helping us to reach our plan. Our plan may need to include major equipment purchases and plant modernization as an integral part.

Adequacy of Goals and Objectives

We may not be meeting our plan as we desire because it is a poor plan. The goals and objectives, which are the heart of the plan, may be poorly set. They may be unrealistically high, written ambiguously, not amenable to measurement, or may require resources far beyond our capabilities to provide.

Thus, a third reason why we may not be reaching our plan, in addition to the performance of people or machines, is a poorly written and communicated plan. This is a common reason for poor performance under the plan, especially for organizations with little experience in the strategic planning process. These problems are normal and should not keep an organization from engaging in the planning process. Usually, better forecasting, assessment, and budgeting will help to bring realism to goals and objectives.

WHAT ARE THE CHARACTERISTICS OF EFFECTIVE CORRECTIVE ACTION?

Corrective action systems are most effective if they are timely, future oriented, positive, and preventive. Let us look at each of these.

Timeliness. A good corrective action system brings performance back on track before it gets too far out of line. When we let things go, hoping that they will "correct themselves," we may create the impression that we condone the present state of affairs. A sales manager who says nothing about a fall off in quarterly sales in a particular region may create the impression that the sales drop is acceptable to the company.

On the other hand, we should not be too quick to correct. Some out-of-line performances will naturally come back on line. If we have conscientious people who are able to monitor their own activities, chances are that they will take action to bring out-of-line performances back on line without us having to say anything. It is a fine line that we must walk in balancing the need for timely corrective action with the danger of exercising too close management control.

Future Orientation. The corrective action system should concentrate on the future, not the past. We want to study the past only so we can avoid making the same mistakes in the future. Dwelling on past mistakes by using "should haves" as in "you should have done this" or "we should have done that" is counterproductive.

Preventive. If we are future oriented, our corrective action systems will be concerned not only with correcting the present problem, but also with preventing it from happening again in the future.

Positive. We want our corrective action system to bring about positive change, not punish past performance. We do not want negative systems. Our systems should be geared to correcting future performance and should stress expected positive performance rather than to dwell, in a negative way, on inadequate past performance.

WHAT TYPES OF CORRECTIVE ACTION SYSTEMS CAN WE USE?

The general guideline states that the best corrective system is self-correcting. Such that when performance gets out of line, the system acts to correct itself. This is the way an automatic pilot works on an airplane. Such cybernetic systems are not always that easy to construct, but there are some actions that we can take to build self-correcting systems.

Any system that is not self-correcting requires outside action to correct it. Outside action usually comes in the form of a management directive, but we can also use policies, procedures, rules, and organization structure as outside mechanisms for corrective action.

Role of Policy. Under strategic planning, the development of organizational policies, procedures, structure, and so on flow from the strategic plan. In other words, the plan dictates policy. Too often, unfortunately, the opposite happens in organizations. Policies are developed for specific situations and they soon assume a life of their own. The reason for their existence and the tie to the accomplishment of objectives never is clear.

Policies are broad guidelines to action. If they are tied to the plan, they help organizational members to achieve the plan. Policy, structure, and procedure too often have the opposite effect—they weigh heavily on the shoulders of organizational participants and actually seem to work against the plan. When this happens we have a situation known as bureaucracy. There is much paper shuffling and rule following, but not much gets accomplished.

Consequently, a major activity of any organization engaging in the strategic planning process is to conduct a policy audit. Existing policies should be reviewed to see if they are helping or hindering the accomplishment of the plan. Those that are hindering should be changed or dropped. Likewise, organization structure may need attention to determine if units should be added, re-focused, or dropped in light of the plan. Procedures should also be reviewed to see if they can be updated and streamlined.

In sum, the strategic plan should drive policy and procedure development and the re-formulation of organization structure. Organizations that fail to develop this necessary tie-in will have great difficulty in making their strategic plan work.

However, as we said earlier, the best corrective systems are self-correcting. How can we develop these kinds of systems?

Self Correcting Systems. We need to get people into our organization who can work with some degree of autonomy and who are willing to take responsibility for their own actions. If we accurately communicate the plan to these people and ensure that tracking information is provided to them accurately and on a timely basis, they will take action to correct deviations in performance without having to be told to do so. If our policies, procedures, and structure are driven by the plan, these people will follow these guidelines to make the plan work. In other words, these outside factors (i.e., policies and procedures) to correct substandard performance will be internalized by the people following the plan and will be used as a basis for self-correcting actions. No one will necessarily have to tell them what to do. They will know, and, if they do not, they will figure it out.

While this is an idealized state of affairs, it makes clear how important it is to have trained, knowledgeable, and competent people in our organization. Making a strategic plan work without competent people will be very difficult. If we do not now have people with these desired characteristics, then an element in our strategic plan should deal with obtaining and developing these kinds of people. We may have to change our recruiting, placement, promotion, and training strategies in order to ensure that we have competent people to carry out the plan.

If we lack competent people and see little way of changing that situation because of restrictive hiring rules caused by a union or civil service system, then we will need to rely more on external corrective action and control. This means our policy, procedure, and structure are likely to become more restrictive by becoming more centralized and by having numerous cross checks. In short, if we are not careful, we will be well on the road to bureaucracy.

Achieving effective corrective action through external means without becoming bureaucratic is, indeed, difficult. This is why in the long run it is best to improve the quality of people in our organization. One distinct benefit of the strategic planning process is that it forces us to give a good hard look at our personnel. We may need to set strategic goals for personnel improvement that deal with a number of facets of the personnel process: setting a competitive wage or salary, instituting a career development program, using better recruiting and selection strategies, and rewarding performance rather than seniority or other variables. These actions will help to attract, keep, and motivate the productive employees we need to make the plan work.

WHAT IS A GOOD FORM TO USE FOR CORRECTIVE ACTION?

Exhibit 46 shows a corrective action form that can be completed when part of the plan seems to be going awry. Notice that the form requires the analyst to be specific as to the performance inadequacy and what needs to be done to improve the situation. Stress is placed on who will do what by when.

Exhibit 47 shows a sample corrective action form for the quality control example objective we have examined several times elsewhere in this

Exhibit 46
Worksheet Form for Corrective Action

CORRECTIVE ACTION FORM

Date_____

Name:_____

Unit:_____

Performance Inadequacy:_____

_____

Related to Objective:_____

_____

Cause of Inadequacy   *Corrective Action*
(List all that apply. Be specific.)

With the Objective: With the Objective:

With Performance: With Performance:

With Plant, Machines, Tools: With Plant, Machines, Tools:

_____

Note: Be sure to specify who will do what by when in the above in order to correct
performance.

book. Notice that the form can be kept short, simple, and to the point
and yet be quite specific. Presumably, in the example shown here, if they
raise the entry salary for two training analyst positions, and use the
Baker Roto Assembly machine to institute the new training process, they
will now be able to institute the new training program that will help them
improve product quality so that they can reach their objective.

WHAT CAN BE DONE TO MAKE THE STRATEGIC
PLAN WORK AND TO ANTICIPATE THE NEEDS FOR
CORRECTIVE ACTION?

Planning fails for many reasons. We have reviewed most of these
reasons elsewhere in the book. Therefore, they will only be summarized
briefly here.

Exhibit 47
Sample Completed Corrective Action Worksheet

Date: *May 22, 1986*

Name: *Jerry Jackson*

Unit: *Training and Development*

Performance Inadequacy : Has not instituted new training procedures in roto area assembly process.

Related to Objective: To reduce quality control rejects by 50 percent by December 31, 1986.

Cause of Inadequacy:	*Corrective Action:*
With the Objective: None. Objective realistic	With the Objective: None.
With Performance: Two training analysts have left and have not been replaced because of low salaries in positions.	With Performance: Personnel raise entry salary level at least 30 percent to attract qualified candidates by June 10, 1986.
With Plant, Machines, Tools: Difficulty in locating a roto simulation.	With Plant, Machines, tools: Production take Baker Roto Assembly machine from line for use in training by June 19, 1986.

- Lack of commitment from top management to initiate the process and see it through.
- Analysis paralysis. We analyze everything to death and don't get on with action.
- Poor environmental scanning and forecasting that does not anticipate crises and emergencies.
- Paperwork overload that chokes and clogs the planning process.
- No time to plan because of work overload caused by a failure to delegate, poor time management, or poorly designed jobs.
- Lack of adequate participation and communication in developing the plan. The plan is autocratically set.
- Rigidity and lack of flexibility in the plan. Once written, the plan appears to be cast in concrete.
- Poorly designed and managed planning workshops. Nothing gets done.
- Failure to perform a key step adequately in the planning model, whether it be the environmental scan, internal assessment, mission formulation, or whatever.
- Failure to assign the strategic planning function to a committee, task force, or group with the interest, competence, and motivation to initiate the activity and see it through.

- Assigning the planning function only to a planning staff and not heavily involving line management.
- Lack of contingency planning to deal with environmental uncertainties.
- Failure to get to specifics: Who will do what by when and how will we know it gets done?
- Failure to tie the planning process to the budgeting process.
- Previous planning efforts may have met with limited success and the participants don't want to get involved again.
- Lack of substance in the plan. The plan deals with tangential and trivial subjects not the real work of the organization.
- Lack of a reward system based on plan performance. People receive pay raises and promotions based upon other factors (e.g., seniority) rather than performance under the plan.
- Lack of a general consensus or agreement on the plan. The plan is discussed over and over but never gets implemented.

Of course there are other factors that can keep a plan from being implemented, but these are the most common ones. The more the above list of factors can be anticipated and actually dealt with in the planning process, the less chance they will come back to thwart plan implementation. The less chance, too, that numerous forms of major corrective action will be needed to make the plan work.

HOW IS CORRECTIVE ACTION RELATED TO PROBLEM SOLVING?

When corrective action is needed, it needs to be taken forcefully. As we said, self-correction is the best. When people take self-correction it needs to pinpoint the problem specifically and address it. In other words, it is important that the problem with performance be accurately defined before action is taken.

Too often we attempt to solve a problem by focusing on its symptoms—manifestations of the problem, not the problem itself. We should be concerned with addressing the cause of the symptoms; this is the problem. If we just treat symptoms and not their causes, we only temporarily "solve" the problem. Until we get at the cause, the problem is likely to manifest itself again, often in a different form.

For example, one retail company had difficulty in reaching an objective of opening new stores on time. The people involved believed it was because the local zoning laws of the various cities were complex and delayed the construction process. Hence, they tried to improve the permit process to get construction started in each city. In reality, the local zoning laws were not causing the problem. The problem was incompetent legal advice. The legal firm being used by the company was not experienced in construction permits. A switch to a more specialized legal firm in the permit process cleared up the problem in a matter of days.

It's tempting to take quick action directed at symptoms without probing the real problem. Probing takes time and effort; many managers are busy and often go for the easy quick fix. While this may solve the problem in the short run, it is not a good long-term strategy. We pay for the quick fix by having to make additional quick fixes until we finally realize we need to get at the basic cause of the problem.

Defining the problem is often a difficult process. The key is to ask the question "why?" enough times so that we are able to peel away the layers of symptoms and superficial problems. If we do this enough, we will eventually get to the root cause of the problem. We may also be surprised to find out that the basic problem not only causes the symptoms we observed but also other symptoms in the company.

For example, a company experiencing high turnover in its factory initially believed it was caused by a low wage rate and hot working conditions. However, after some analysis, they found that the high turnover rate was being caused by very poor supervisory practices. Most of the supervisors had been promoted from within and had not received any on-the-job or classroom supervisory training. A comprehensive training program for supervisors soon corrected the turnover problem.

A worksheet form for problem analysis appears in Exhibit 48. Of course, it is not only useful to use this form in the corrective action phase of planning, but also in the internal assessment phase where we are interested in determining the strengths and weaknesses of the organization. Using the form in the assessment phase will help us to pinpoint our problems better so that we can write proper objectives to correct them.

Exhibit 48
Worksheet Form for Analyzing Problems

PROBLEM ANALYSIS FORM

1. Problem Symptoms (How do we know we have a problem?)————————

——

——

2. How did we become aware of the symptoms?————————————————

——

——

Exhibit 48 (Continued)

3. Is the problem related to this objective?_____

    _____

    _____

4. Why/how do we know the symptoms actually exist? Are we sure we really
    have a problem?_____

    _____

    _____

5. What appears to be the cause of the symptoms?_____

    _____

    _____

6. What other factors could be causing the symptoms?_____

    _____

    _____

7. What appears to be the one basic cause?_____

    _____

    _____

8. What can we do to alleviate this cause?_____

    _____

Strategic planning is a deceptively simple process. Most organizations
today have tried some form of strategic planning. Many have had a bitter
experience with the process and do not wish to attempt it again.

In other organizations when strategic planning is mentioned by an
outside consultant, a common response is "we already are doing most of
that." In fact, what they may already be doing is a type of hit or miss, ad
hoc type of planning—not the comprehensive, systematic, logical type of

strategic planning discussed in this book. However, if an organization is doing some planning, it often can be easier to expand it to full-blown strategic planning than if it is doing no planning at all. At least they have a start.

For an organization just beginning the strategic planning process, it can take a long time until the process is fully implemented. The process is considered fully implemented when the following happens:

1. The plan is used daily by managers and discussed at management and board meetings.
2. The plan is tied to the budget.
3. The plan is tied to the appraisal and reward system.

Estimates vary but many experts in the field believe it takes from three to five years to implement the strategic planning process fully in an organization that is doing little if any planning at present. I've found this to be the case in my experience.

Of course, even though it may take three to five years to implement the strategic planning process fully, this should not discourage a firm from beginning the process by adopting a few of the more basic steps. For example, the three key steps of determining a mission, developing objectives, and writing action steps can be implemented first. As the participants become more familiar with the process, other steps can be added.

Also, even though strategic planning is geared to the top executive level, the head of a division or other similar unit should not avoid planning simply because there is no organization-wide strategic plan. While it is true that it is easier to develop and implement a divisional strategic plan if an organization-wide plan exists, it is not true that a division cannot proceed to develop a plan in the absence of a corporate-wide plan. I've worked with a number of organizations at the divisional level in developing a strategic plan and, if done properly, by and large they have been successful. In fact, some companies not now engaging in the strategic planning process will experiment with it at the divisional level prior to adopting the process organization-wide.

There are often bitterly disappointing periods in the planning process. People are usually excited in the initial stages of planning. They see it as a potentially very useful tool in helping them to manage their operations and their time. However, after a few setbacks (e.g., missed deadlines) they begin to become disenchanted. The honeymoon is over. It is important that the commitment is there from the top to get the organization through these disappointing periods. Without this commitment—this push—the people involved will view strategic planning as a passing fad and wait for it to go away. It will be another tool dropped on the scrap heap of passing management fads.

Even though strategic planning is a very challenging process, it can be fun and very rewarding from a personal standpoint. At my workshop sessions I've heard comments such as, "This is the first time we've really communicated about important things," "This is the first time we really got to the nitty-gritty instead of just talking," and "I really feel good now that I have a clear sense of direction." The plan can give structure where little existed, guidance for a foundering organization, and a clear sense of purpose or mission to bind organizational efforts. Many organizations have moved from mediocracy to high levels of success by adopting strategic planning. It is a proven way of achieving excellence.

The next section of the book contains an actual strategic plan. The company is a real company but its name and selected other facts have been changed to ensure confidentiality. Many people want to see what the finished product looks like. While the actual finished plan varies greatly from company to company, the plan for Spina's is an excellent example of a comprehensive strategic plan.

Part III

An Example of Strategic Planning

The last part of the book presents an actual strategic plan for a food service company. Based on an actual company the name and other identifying factors have been changed to protect client confidentiality.

This plan is exemplary not only because of its perfection in every detail, but also because of its fluidity and succinctness. One does not have to be in the food service or restaurant business to learn from this case. The kinds of decisions that were made in this case are similar to those made by all companies, although the contexts may be different.

15.

The Strategic Plan of Spina's Food

Spina's Fine Foods, Inc., is a restaurant chain and food processor specializing primarily in high-quality Italian foods. The company operates primarily in Georgia. It has a central food-processing plant in Atlanta where it prepares frozen Italian dishes for sale in grocery stores throughout the Atlanta area. It also has four restaurants located in medium-sized towns in Georgia that specialize in Italian dishes.

BACKGROUND

The company was founded in 1979 by the Spina family. It began with a small restaurant in Macon, Georgia. The restaurant emphasizes fresh, not frozen, Italian dishes prepared in the middle to northern Italian style. This style emphasizes a lighter tomato sauce and more white sauces than the traditional Italian restaurants found in most American cities. While this different style had become popular in New York, Chicago, and a few other larger cities, it was largely untried in medium-sized towns until Spina's began.

The first restaurant was opened in 1979 in a small, high-quality luxury shopping mall of specialty shops in Macon, Georgia. The restaurant itself was small, seating 75 people. It featured intimate dining in a tastefully decorated atmosphere of linen table cloths, candlelight, fresh flowers, plants, and quality fixtures. Service was professional and personal. The restaurant contrasted with the typical Mom and Pop Italian restaurants of the checkered oil cloth variety popular throughout the South.

The success of the first restaurant led to the opening of a second restaurant in Albany, Georgia, in 1981. It followed the same basic strategy as the first—high quality, small regional mall location, etc.—and it met with success. Since then, two additional restaurants have been opened in Valdosta and Athens, Georgia. All have followed the same basic formula and have been successful.

The food-processing plant began in 1984. Initially, the company produced only noodles and canned sauces. These were shipped to the restaurants. However, the company is now experimenting with frozen foods for retail distribution and has three items: lasagna, manicotti, and lemony scallopini. So far, sales are through supermarkets only in the Atlanta area but sales levels have been very encouraging. The frozen dishes are not shipped to the restaurants. The restaurants still emphasize fresh food preparation of all dishes.

The company is headed by Richard Spina, who is founder, principal owner, and president. Richard is 36 years old. The majority of stock is owned by the Spina family. William, Richard's brother, shares ownership with Philip and Amelia, their mother and father. However, there are five outside shareholders who hold a minority (40 percent) of the stock. They were brought into the company initially because the family wished to raise sufficient capital to ensure a high-quality first restaurant. Other key employees of the company include Walt Alexander, manager of the food-processing factory; Jeff Zambelli, controller; and Fred Pezzoli, Jim Hogg, Anita Sebastian, and Tom Carroll, restaurant managers.

The company has some outstanding debt in the form of a partially used line of credit from an Atlanta bank. Virtually all growth has been fueled by retained earnings and new stock issues to present shareholders. The company's pre-tax annual return on investment has averaged 35 percent for the past six years. Annual pre-tax return to investors has averaged 20 percent, in the form of dividends.

All buildings are leased in the shopping centers. The factory is also leased. All equipment has been purchased. Each shopping center site and the factory required a substantial investment in leasehold improvements by the company.

CURRENT ISSUES

The company has done little formal strategic planning in the past. However, since it has grown rapidly and sees future rapid growth, Richard believes the development of a formal strategic plan is now a must. Richard believes there is substantial profit opportunity in expanding both the food-processing and restaurant operations. However, he realizes that there is some disagreement among the owners as to the type of expansion desired. Some have argued for franchising. Others wish to expand just food processing. Still others wish to get into the fast-food/carryout line with Italian foods.

Richard believes the company is at a turning point in its development. It can either remain a small, profitable, state-wide operation, or it can expand rapidly into a national corporation. If such expansion is desirable the issue thus becomes: What form should this expansion take? Should the company simply continue with its proven method of success by continuing to add small- to medium-sized restaurants in small towns and by expanding food production, or should the company expand through entirely different means such as fast-food franchising? Richard hoped that the development of a comprehensive strategic plan would answer these questions.

THE PLANNING PROCESS

The company now operates with a formal budget. Annual reviews are made of company performance and general objectives are set. However, comprehensive strategic planning is not now done. Richard decided to set aside a long weekend at St. Simons Island, Georgia for a planning retreat. The retreat would be conducted by Dr. Ron Reynolds, a group facilitator in strategic planning.

The retreat was held from Friday noon until Sunday afternoon. The agenda was as follows:

Friday

12:00–1:00	lunch
1:00–2:00	overview of the strategic planning process
2:00–2:15	break
2:15–3:15	environmental analysis
3:15–4:15	environmental forecasting
4:15–5:00	environmental opportunities and constraints
5:00–7:00	cocktails and dinner
7:00–9:00	customer/market profile

Saturday

9:00–10:00	planning premises and assumptions
10:00–11:00	mission statement
11:00–12:00	objectives
12:00– 1:00	lunch
1:00– 4:00	objectives
4:00– 5:00	action steps

Sunday

9:00–12:00	action steps, scheduling, accountability, tracking
12:00– 2:00	budgeting (tentative)
2:00	adjournment

Prior to the meeting, the participants were given material to read on the strategic planning process and were asked to draft a possible mission statement for the company. They were invited to bring family to the resort, but family were not permitted in the planning sessions.

As the session progressed, Ron, the group facilitator, made notes on large flip chart sheets and taped them to the walls. After the session, these sheets were reviewed and a tentative plan was developed based upon the material on the sheets.

Richard believes the session went well and that the typed plan presents the company with a useful working document. Most of the plan the company developed is reproduced on the following pages.

SPINA'S STRATEGIC PLAN FOR 1986–1991 PLANNING PERIOD

Environmental Scan

Exhibit 49 is a matrix of Spina's environment.

Economy. The economy of Georgia and contiguous states is diversified and strong. Manufacturing, service, government, and military-related sectors are growing rapidly. The farming sector is becoming more mechanized and sophisticated. Labor is abundant and relatively low cost.

Competition. Competition from similar, specialized ethnic restaurants is growing, particularly in the larger towns. Chains such as Bennigans are also growing, even in medium-sized towns. Mom and Pop Italian restaurants are stable to stagnant. Competition from Stouffers and others for frozen specialized foods is also growing.

Legal/Political. The legal environment in the area favors business growth. The relaxation of drinking control laws has made beer, wine, and to some extent hard liquor more readily available in medium-sized Southern towns.

Social. The area has increased in social sophistication. Dining out at more fashionable restaurants has become more accepted as opposed to just eating "on the run." The spread of two-career families has made dining out more convenient and affordable. It has also enhanced the acceptance of higher-priced frozen dinners.

Demographics. The medium-sized cities in the region are growing rapidly, primarily through net migration as new industry moves south and as government and military expenditures expand.

Technology. Restaurant food service and preparation have increasingly become automated through new and faster equipment, such as microwave and convection ovens, standardization, and specialization. Cooking from standardized high-quality recipes using fresh ingredients is becoming more widely adopted.

Labor Market. The labor market for food service workers is very good in the medium-sized towns and in Atlanta. Many students and others looking for part-time work come to these towns from more rural areas. Wage rates are relatively low. Unions are scarce, although more common in Atlanta.

Key Physical Resources. Exclusive shopping centers are a real plus in terms of attractiveness and location. The plant is old but all the equipment is practically new. Interior decoration of restaurants is very attractive with wall coverings, high-quality carpeting, furnishings, and fixtures.

Suppliers. Some limitation on a few specialty items. Otherwise, suppliers are growing in number and competitiveness as to price and service.

Distributors. Distributors of processed food are becoming more competitive due to trucking deregulation. Major grocery store chains seem receptive to product.

Transportation. Reliable transportation readily available throughout region.

Energy Supplies. Energy supply in areas of operation appear to be abundant.

International Conditions. At this time, no effect on business.

Environmental Forecast

The environmental forecast for Spina's is very favorable and is conducive to continued vigorous growth for the firm. The forecast shows strong economic and population growth in targeted cities in the South-

Exhibit 49
Spina's Environmental Analysis

Opportunities	Constraints
Growing labor market for part-time work	Increasing costs to finance and build plant expansion and restaurants
Expanding economy	Potential competition from processed foods maker and similar restaurants
Expanding two-career families	Potential inflation of food costs
Desire to "trade up" both in dining out and processed food	
Limited competition	
Increasing technology in food service and preparation	

eastern United States. Population levels, annual increases in family income, labor availability, good energy and water availability, stable land and building costs, and more diversified suppliers all will provide opportunities for continued growth. A more sophisticated dining public will create opportunities to market both the restaurants and frozen food lines.

With this opportunity will come increased competition as other restauranteurs and food-processing firms attempt to tap the market. Stouffers and several other frozen food processors are already marketing a line of frozen foods geared to the top end of the market. Several restaurant chains such as General Foods' Olive Garden Italian Restaurants are making inroads in the up-scale Italian restaurant market.

Consequently, the company interprets this forecast to mean that many environmental opportunities are available in both restaurants and food processing, but action will need to be taken quickly in order to beat the competition before they obtain a strong position in the market.

The forecast prepared by the company, with some outside assistance, follows:

Economy. Favorable economic conditions for the entire Southeast and its medium-sized cities should continue as the Sunbelt continues to enjoy strong industrial expansion as a result of northern and midwestern manufacturing firms moving south. The annual inflation rate for these cities should average one to two percentage points below the national rate. Unemployment rates should remain below national levels. Interest rates are likely to be slightly above national levels as pressure is placed on available funding in order to fuel growth.

Competition. Increased competition from up-scale restaurants, especially chains such as Bennigans, Ruby Tuesdays, Olive Garden, and others is likely to become intense as these firms recognize the growth potential of medium-sized southern cities. In addition, independent up-scale restaurants featuring continental and Italian cuisine are likely to become more common. Competition in processed foods from Stouffers, Banquet, and others is likely to increase as they come out with high-quality, high-priced frozen entrees.

Legal/Political. The legal and political climate in the Southeast is favorable for continued business expansion at both the state and local level. The availability of both wine and food and beverage (alcohol) licenses in medium-sized cities is expected to be good. Zoning laws are favorable to business.

Social. A more sophisticated dining customer is emerging in the medium-sized southern city. As more northerners move south because plants have closed or because of retirement and as incomes continue to expand, especially those of two-income families, the desired dining experience is likely to be more sophisticated. Candlelight, wine, table cloths, fine food and service, and a pleasant atmosphere are likely to be a more desired part of the dining experience. In addition, ethnic foods are popular with the dining public. Chinese, Mexican, and Italian foods are the three most popular ethnic foods and are growing in popularity each year. Finally, social mores and small families are making frozen foods, especially high-quality entrees, more acceptable and affordable for home evening meals.

Demographic. Population increases in mid-sized southern cities are predicted to be quite strong. Increases in the 22 to 45 age group—the prime dining out group—are forecasted to be very good as the "baby boom" matures. Dual-career families will continue to grow as career opportunities and social mores continue to make it more acceptable for women to hold jobs outside the home. High-quality regional shopping centers will expand rapidly. There will be fewer enclosed large shopping malls built in mid-sized southern cities since a saturation point for this type of shopping center has been reached at least on a temporary basis.

Technology. The technology of restaurant food preparation will continue to focus on developing fast, low-energy-use equipment. Convection and microwave ovens will continue to dominate. Standardization of restaurant operations through the use of standardized recipes and operating manuals will expand. The use of computers for cashiering, inventory control, bookkeeping, and payroll will continue to expand. The technology in factory food processing will become less labor intensive as more automated processing lines, including the use of computers and robotics, become available to food processors. Techniques for storing and freezing foods will continue to be developed, which will improve freshness and taste while reducing spoilage. More widespread use of microwave ovens in homes will make frozen entrees easier to prepare. There will be less stigma attached to microwave oven usage as the taste and nutrition of frozen entrees improve.

Labor Market. The labor market of the Atlanta area is good and conducive to plant expansion. There will likely be a shortage of skilled food processors who have a knowledge of computers. The labor market for restaurant help in mid-sized cities is likely to remain tight, particularly for cooks. However, most cities have a college, university, or community college that provides a large pool of part-time restaurant employees. Standardized recipes and operating manuals will make it easier to train available employees for restaurant operations.

Energy Supplies. Few if any energy shortages are projected for the region for the next three to five years. Electricity and natural gas costs are projected to increase about 10 percent per year. Water is abundant in the area.

Key Physical Resources. The availability of high-quality regional mall space is expected to increase. Room is available for plant expansion at the present site.

Suppliers. Restaurant suppliers in mid-sized southern towns are limited, especially with certain Italian items such as special noodles, Italian sausage, specialty meats (e.g., prosciutto), and fresh fish. However, as these cites grow, additional suppliers should begin to service the region. Suppliers for food processing in Atlanta are many and varied. No shortages are anticipated here.

Distributors. Distributors for processed food are readily available and will continue to be so.

Transportation. Available sites in mid-sized southern towns can be found adjacent or near major roads. Transportation by truck of frozen items is good and will continue to be so.

International Conditions. Not anticipated to affect operations.

Customer/Market Analysis

Spina's has two primary markets. The first is that segment of the public that desires to enjoy a high-quality dining experience outside of the home. The second is that segment of the public that wishes to enjoy a high-quality dining experience, conveniently prepared, within the home. Both groups enjoy Italian food made with the highest quality, fresh ingredients carefully prepared and attractively served whether in the home or at a restaurant. However, they do not want the mess and bother of extensive preparation. They want convenience. The Customer Profile in Exhibit 50 shows a market that is changing and growing.

Strategic Planning Premises and Assumptions

After careful review of the environmental assessment, environmental forecast, and customer/market analysis, Spina's developed the following strategic planning premises and key assumptions:

1. The popularity of high-quality Italian food will continue to increase significantly during the next few years throughout most of the southeastern United States.

2. Mid-sized southeastern cities will continue to experience much growth as more northern and midwestern firms relocate to the sunbelt. This relocation will increase the professional and managerial occupational classes in these cities.

3. Chain competitors will expand in the larger southeastern cities and will avoid the mid-sized ones for the next year or two.

4. Processed high-quality Italian food items will expand in demand. However, there will be strong competition in the market from Stouffers, Banquet, and other food processors.

5. People will continue to desire strongly a high-quality dining experience in an intimate setting and will be willing to pay a premium price for it.

Exhibit 50
Customer Profile

		Yesterday	Today	Tomorrow
Demographic				
Age:	Restaurants:	22–45	24–50	24–65
	Processed Foods:	22–30	22–35	22–40
Income:	Restaurants:	$15,000/year	$25,000/year	$35,000/year
	Processed Foods:	20,000/year	25,000/year	30,000/year
Education:	Restaurants:	14 years	15 years	16 years
	Processed Foods:	14 years	15 years	15 years
Geographic:	Restaurants:	Few medium cities	Several medium cities	Southern medium cities with high concentration of professionals
	Processed Foods:	Large city	Medium and large cities	Medium and large cities
Family Size:	Restaurants:	2.2	2.5	3
	Processed Foods:	2	2.5	3
Other:		Gourmets; well-traveled people	Professional occupations; well traveled	Professional and managerial occupations; well traveled; large to medium city rearing
Psychological				
Needs:		Status, prestige, convenience, service	Same	Same
Wants:		Tasty food, impress clients/friends; recognized by manager, personal attention	Same	Same with more attention to health and nutritional value of food

Exhibit 50 (Continued)

PROJECTED MARKET GROWTH:

Existing markets:	10 percent per year with existing restaurants and processed food line.
New markets:	50 percent per year potential by opening two restaurants per year and adding more processed items.
Competitor markets:	None. Not much competition in potential cities.
Other factors:	Need to educate potential market on value and taste of high quality Italian items. "More veal, less spaghetti."
	Need to concentrate in cities where major chains (e.g., Olive Garden) are not likely to locate.

---

6. The Atlanta area will continue to be a prime location for a food-processing plant because of its abundant labor market, excellent transportation system, and ready availability of raw foodstuffs.

Internal Assessment

Spina's used the short version of survey feedback technique to complete the internal assessment. Using the data gathered from the survey plus available financial data, the strengths and weaknesses chart (Exhibit 51) was completed during the workshop session of the strategic planning participants. Spina's believes that the collective pooled judgment of these people, backed up by data from the survey and financial data, enabled the company to develop an accurate picture of the strengths and weaknesses of the company.

Mission

The mission of Spina's has evolved as it has grown. Initially, the mission was to begin and operate one high-quality Italian restaurant in Macon, Georgia. Soon, two other restaurants were added as was the food-processing plant.

Now, poised at a critical juncture in its growth cycle, a new mission has been formed: to profitably operate a chain of high-quality, intimate Italian restaurants in medium-sized cities throughout the southeastern United States and to operate an Italian food processing plant profitably with southeastern distribution of items.

Exhibit 51
Internal Assessment: Strengths and Weaknesses of Spina's

	Strengths	Weaknesses
Personnel	Generally high-quality cooking and server staff because of the use of aggressive college-aged students who have been properly trained. Food-processing plant has generally adequate employees.	Not enough skilled people in top management. This is true of both restaurants and food plant. High turnover rate of restaurant employees.
Products	Both restaurant and food processing products are viewed by the public as having the highest of quality because of fresh, high-quality ingredients and careful preparation.	Restaurant items are often viewed as heavy and high in calories by some customers.
Operations	The use of procedure manuals both in the restaurants and plant make for uniform and generally smooth operations.	Temporary emergencies sometimes experienced in the restaurant when people unexpectedly quit or do not show up for their shift.
Finances	Low debt and high investment of retained earnings has enabled the company to achieve a moderate rate of growth.	Present financial structure will not support rapid growth.
Physical Facilities	Restaurants are in existing attractive locations and are attractively decorated and furnished. Plant is modern.	Some kitchens of early restaurants are crowded. Major remodeling of existing restaurants will be needed within the next two years.
Equipment	Restaurant equipment is current and state of the art.	Plant equipment can be modernized, especially if production expands.
Location	The strategy of locating restaurants in small, high-quality malls in medium-sized southern cities appears to be appropriate. Plant in good location in Atlanta.	Leasing does not allow enough asset formulation in the business.

Exhibit 51 (Continued)

	Strengths	Weaknesses
Management	Very top management of company is knowledgeable and well trained. Plant management is generally good throughout.	Restaurant managers and assistant managers are generally inexperienced and occasionally not highly motivated. There is excessive dependence on the expertise of Richard Spina, CEO.
Research and Development	This is generally good in both the plant and restaurants. New menu items are experimented with via specials in restaurants. Entire menu is revised at least twice a year.	More research and development in tasty, low calorie, high nutrition restaurant meals is needed.
Customer Services/Image	The firm enjoys a very good reputation with a loyal (repeat) customer base. "The customer is always right" is a guiding principle in the restaurant. Complimentary dinner and drinks are provided without question if a customer is dissatisfied.	Occasional delays occur in serving meals, especially if an emergency occurs because of an unforeseen quit or someone fails to show for a shift. Image of processed food is not as strong as restaurant image.
Special Assets/Problems	The principal owner and CEO, Richard Spina, is viewed as a strong asset by the entire company. Recipes are secret and viewed as a special asset.	None.

Strategic Thrusts

The strategic thrusts for Spina's for the next three to five years are as follows:

1. to have a public offering of stock to raise $1 million for expansion
2. to open one new restaurant every nine months in mid-sized southern towns

3. to provide equity ownership for restaurant managers and assistant managers
4. to double the number of items and production level at the food plant
5. to begin and complete a program of converting from leases to ownership of old and new restaurants and the plant

Objectives

The following objectives and respective rationales were developed for Spina's five strategic thrusts:

STRATEGIC THRUST:
To have a public offering of stock to raise $1 million for expansion.
OBJECTIVES:
1. To construct the offering so as to maintain control by the present investors.
Rationale: Present investors, especially the family wish to maintain control of the entire operation.
2. To complete the offering by September 1, 1986.
Rationale: Need to complete early so expansion can begin as soon as possible.
3. To provide the offering primarily in Georgia, Alabama, and South Carolina through personal contact.
Rationale: Need to keep fees as low as possible. Want to involve present investors in making the offering.

STRATEGIC THRUST:
To open a new restaurant every nine months in mid-sized southern towns.
OBJECTIVES:
1. To conduct feasibility analysis and locate five key cities for expansion by December 31, 1986.
Rationale: Towns that match desired demographics with high-quality malls are targets for expansion efforts.
2. To open a new restaurant every nine months beginning September 1, 1987.
Rationale: A schedule for opening restaurants is needed that allows spacing for training and break-in time.
3. To duplicate present restaurants at each new one opened.
Rationale: Present concept is successful.
4. To provide uniformity of training and operations in each restaurant beginning with the first new one.
Rationale: Present training manuals need to be revised and more firmly enforced to reduce minor variances in service and food quality.

STRATEGIC THRUST:
To provide equity ownership for restaurant managers and assistant managers.
OBJECTIVES:
1. To structure and implement a procedure to allow existing restaurant managers and assistant managers to acquire ownership in their particular

restaurant at a 25 percent amount for managers and at a 15 percent amount for assistant managers by June 1, 1987.

Rationale: Ownership should enhance the professionalism and incentives for performance of restaurant management.

2. To implement the stock ownership plan in new restaurants within one year after they are in operation.

Rationale: Restaurant management should demonstrate one year of performance before ownership is permitted.

STRATEGIC THRUST:
To double the number of items and production level at the food plant.
OBJECTIVES:

1. To add three new food items to production by September 1, 1986.

Rationale: Three popular items will be added based upon market research to expand sales.

2. To expand distribution network by 50 percent by December 1, 1986.

Rationale: Sales expansion can be achieved by adding new markets.

3. To expand production volume by 100 percent at existing plant facility by adding a second shift by December 1, 1986.

Rationale: Better use can be made of existing plant and equipment.

4. To increase advertising program and expenditures by 50 percent by March 1, 1987.

Rationale: Increased advertising will be needed in new markets.

STRATEGIC THRUST:
To begin and complete a program of converting from leases to ownership of restaurants and the plant.
OBJECTIVES:

1. To examine all present leases and determine procedure for terminating leases without penalty by September 1, 1986.

Rationale: Costs and clauses of present leases must be clearly depicted before action taken.

2. To attempt to purchase all existing facilities by December 1, 1986.

Rationale: Condominium ownership in shopping centers is becoming more common. Plant may be purchaseable. Substantial tax and equity advantages to ownership.

3. To locate new facilities for those not purchased by February 1, 1987.

Rationale: Alternative sites must be available before leases terminated.

4. To enter into condominium or free-standing arrangements (next to high-quality mall) for all new restaurants beginning with the first.

Rationale: Substantial tax and equity advantages exist with ownership. Public stock offering should provide the financial resources needed.

Action Steps and Schedules

Since the action steps and schedule for each objective should be developed by those responsible for accomplishing the objective, only a sample of objectives and action steps from Spina's plan are presented (see Exhibits 52–55). Each objective in the plan has action steps and a schedule. Most action steps in the plan also have a number of substeps that were developed by the person responsible for each one. Spina's used the tie-in sheet for each objective. They also used Gantt and PERT charts for some objectives as appropriate.

Exhibit 52
Action Step Tie-in Worksheet for Restaurant Opening Objective

OBJECTIVE: To open a new restaurant every nine months beginning September 1, 1987.

Action Steps	Date for Completion	Person Accountable	Tracking System
1. Locate site for first expansion restaurant in desired city	3/1/87	Richard Spina	Board report
2. Begin site construction / improvements.	3/15/87	Philip Spina	Report to Richard Spina
3. Complete site construction / improvements	6/15/87	Philip Spina	Report to Richard Spina
4. Furnish restaurant.	7/15/87	Amelia Spina	Report to Richard Spina
5. Appoint manager, assistant manager, and training crew	8/1/87	Richard Spina	Board report
6. Hire employees	8/15/87	Restaurant manager	Report to Richard Spina
7. Train employees	9/1/87	Manager and Richard Spina	Observation
8. Open restaurant.	9/1/87	Manager and Richard Spina	Report to board
9. Begin advertising program.	9/1/87	Manager	Observation
10. Hold grand opening.	9/15/87	Manager	Report to Richard Spina
11. Repeat above in sequence for each new restaurant so as to open each restaurant on the following dates:	5/1/88 1/1/89 9/1/89	Manager and Richard Spina	Report to Richard Spina Board report

Exhibit 53
Gantt (Bar) Chart for New Restaurant Openings

Activity

1. Site location

2. Site construction

3. Furnish restaurant

4. Appoint manager and assistant

5. Hire employees

6. Train employees

7. Open restaurant

8. Begin advertising

9. Grand opening

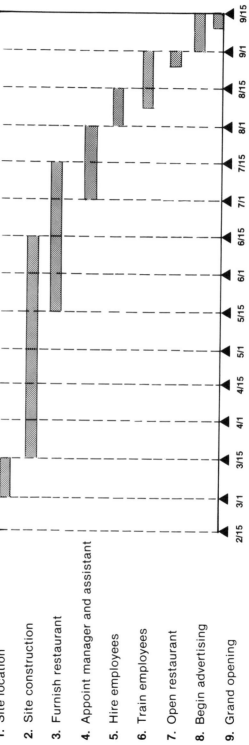

Exhibit 54
Action Step Tie-in Worksheet for Adding New Food Items at Plant

OBJECTIVE: To add three new food items to production by September 1, 1986.

Action Steps	Date for Completion	Person Accountable	Tracking System
1. Do competitive analysis.	2/1/86	William Spina	Report
2. Do consumer research.	4/1/86	Consultant	Report
3. Select three items.	4/15/86	Richard Spina	Report
4. Establish production procedure.	5/15/86	Walt Alexander	Staff meeting
5. Develop packaging	6/15/86	Consultant	Demonstration
6. Begin production.	7/1/86	Walt Alexander	Observation
7. Select test markets.	7/15/86	Consultant	Meeting
8. Advertise.	7/15/86	Richard Spina	Observation
9. If not successful, re-formulate product and re-test until successful.	8/15/86	Richard Spina	Sales report
10. If successful, expand into entire distribution network.	9/1/86	Richard Spina	Meeting

Budgeting

Spina's budgeting process has gradually become more formal with the passing of each year. At the time of the formulation of the present five-year plan, Spina's was on incremental budgeting. A basic operating budget is set and then a budget is built around additional objectives. This additional budget is then added to the basic operating budget.

Because of limited space, only the additional budget created by the previous two objectives is presented in Exhibits 56 and 57.

Standards

Spina's attributes much of its success to high-quality standards in food processing, preparation, and service. Performance standards exist for all positions at the restaurant and most positions in the plant. Standards of freshness, quality, taste, and visual appeal exist for all food items whether prepared in the restaurant or in the plant. Standards of clean-

Exhibit 55
PERT Chart for New Food Items

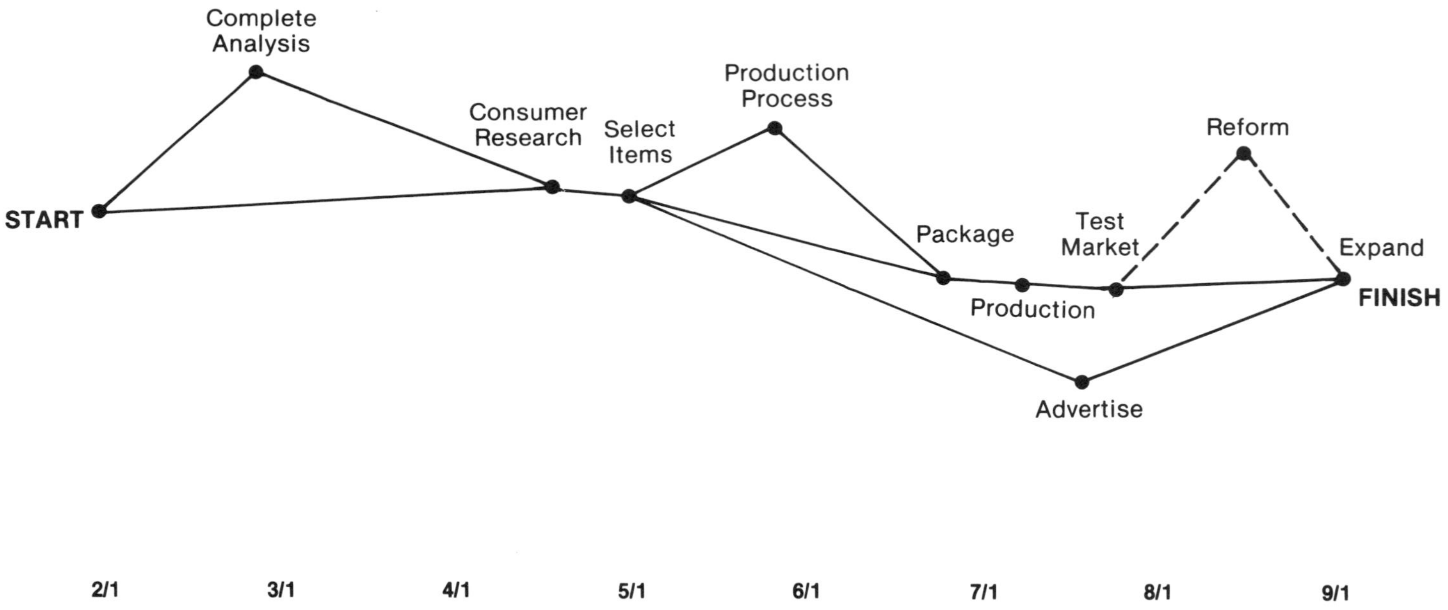

Exhibit 56
Budgeting Tie-in Sheet for Restaurant Openings

OBJECTIVE: To open a new restaurant every nine months beginning
September 1, 1987.

Action Steps	Completion Date	Person Accountable	Tracking	Cost
1. Locate site for first expansion restaurant.	3/1/87	R. Spina	Board report	$101,000
2. Begin site construction / improvements.	3/15/87	P. Spina	Report to R. Spina	5,000
3. Complete site construction / improvements.	6/15/87	P. Spina	Report to R. Spina	45,000
4. Furnish restaurant.	7/15/87	A. Spina	Report to R. Spina	35,000
5. Appoint manager, assistant manager, and training crew.	8/1/87	R. Spina	Board report	500
6. Hire employees.	8/15/87	Restaurant manager	Report to R. Spina	1,000
7. Train employees.	9/1/87	Manager and R. Spina	Observation	5,000
8. Open restaurant.	9/1/87	Manager and R. Spina	Board report	1,000
9. Begin ad program.	9/1/87	Manager	Observation	5,000
10. Grand opening.	9/15/87	Manager	Report to R. Spina	2,000
11. Repeat above for each new restaurant.	5/1/88 1/1/89 9/1/89	R. Spina	Board report	205,500

liness exist for the plant and restaurants. Service standards exist for the
hostesses, waiters/waitresses, busers, and others who meet and serve the
public.

Standards were also formulated for the various objectives that were
formulated in the plan. These standards dealt with time benchmarks and
with restaurant location, layout, and furnishings. Because of the large

volume of standards, only a portion of applicable standards are presented in this section. Representative standards from the plant and restaurants as well as standards for the previous two objectives are presented.

OBJECTIVE: To open a new restaurant every nine months beginning September 1, 1987.

Standards for Restaurant:

1. Located in or adjacent to high-quality small (20,000 square feet) mall in or near an upper middle-class neighborhood on or near major corridors.
2. Restaurant approximately 2,500 square feet in size.
3. Approximately 25 tables in restaurant seating 80 people.
4. Intimate atmosphere:
   • subdued lighting
   • candles and fresh flowers on each table

Exhibit 57
Budgeting Tie-in Sheet for Producing New Food Items

OBJECTIVE: To add three new food items to production by September 1, 1986.

Action Steps	Completion Date	Person Accountable	Tracking	Cost
1. Competitive analysis.	2/1/86	W. Spina	Report	$ 500
2. Consumer research.	4/1/86	Consultant	Report	5,000
3. Select three items.	4/15/86	R. Spina	Report	–
4. Establish production procedure.	5/15/86	W. Alexander	Staff Meeting	5,000
5. Develop packaging.	6/15/86	Consultant	Demonstration	5,000
6. Begin production.	7/1/86	W. Alexander	Observation	15,000
7. Select test markets.	7/15/86	Consultant	Meeting	2,000
8. Advertise.	7/15/86	R. Spina	Observation	25,000
9. Re-formulate if not successful.	8/15/86	R. Spina	Meeting	–
10. If successful, expand into entire distribution network.	9/1/86	R. Spina	Sales report	10,000

- linen tablecloths and napkins
- brass rails with curtains
- three-room division; no more than nine tables in a room
- modern, colorful, framed prints on wall
- burgundy and cream color combination
- many hanging plants
- high-quality carpeting

5. Exterior
   - quality "hours open" sign
   - extensive exterior landscaping including flowers, grass, and trees
   - brick or natural wood veneer
   - paved parking for 50 cars
   - at least two tables and chair sets outside with decorative wine umbrellas
   - awning over door entrance with "Spina's" imprinted

OBJECTIVE: To add three new food items to production by September 1, 1986.

Standards for Food Items:

1. Fresh not frozen ingredients. Used within 24 hours of delivery.
2. Large portion (ounces vary as to items).
3. Each item must generate minimum of $500,000 annual sales.
4. All health code standards must be met in plant at all times.
5. Fresh frozen within 30 minutes of preparation.
6. Shipped within two days of processing.
7. Packaging shows prepared item, properly garnished and served.
8. Item must hold in supermarket and in home freezer for a total of six weeks with no deterioration.
9. Food ingredient cost cannot exceed 20 percent of total marginal cost of preparation and shipping.
10. Food items must be preparable using assembly-line technology.

Restaurant Standards of Customer Service

1. Each customer greeted at door with "Hello, welcome to Spina's. Do you have a reservation?"
2. Customers with reservations seated within 10 minutes of reservation time or a free glass of wine is provided to each person. If wait extends beyond 30 minutes, a free meal is provided to one of the customers in the party.
3. Customers without reservations are to be told of waiting time until seating and are to be seated in waiting area or outside. Drink order taken immediately.

4. Waiters/waitresses are to greet each customer within five mintues of seating as follows: "Hello, My name is _____. Today's specials are _____, _____, etc. I'll be back in a couple of minutes to take your drink order." Customers in restaurant are to receive drink within five minutes of seating (order taken, prepared, and served).

5. Wines are to be properly served (uncorking, wine tasting, customer approval, serve).

6. Food orders are to be taken and served within 20 minutes of seating. All orders served within 5 minutes of preparation.

7. Check presented to customers within five minutes of dinner completion and change or credit card returned within three minutes.

8. Table is to be bused and re-set within five minutes of customer leaving. Chairs wiped and floor swept.

9. Water in glasses is to be kept full at all times.

10. Dishes are to be promptly removed after each course. Courses are to be served as follows: appetizer, salad, main course, dessert and coffee.

11. Customers who order coffee or iced tea are to be given unlimited refills.

12. Tables are to have fresh flowers, lighted candles, and clean table cloth at all times.

13. Waiter/waitress dress is to be white tux shirt, black bow tie, black slacks or skirt, black shoes and socks.

14. Waiters/waitresses are to be clean and well groomed.

15. Bathrooms are to be kept sparkling clean with enough toilet paper, paper towels, and soap. Bathrooms to be checked hourly by busers.

16. Salt, pepper, sugar, and sweetener are to be checked and refilled if necessary after each customer.

17. Maitre d' is to check with each table at least once during the main course to check on meal satisfaction. Dissatisfied customers receive either a free glass of wine or meal depending upon level of dissatisfaction.

18. Customers are to be acknowledged when they leave with "Hope you enjoyed your meal. Please come back."

Restaurant Standards: Food and Beverage Preparation

1. Only fresh ingredients are to be used in all meals—within 48 hours of delivery.

2. Items not served on day of preparation are to be refrigerated and served to employees next day.

3. Orders are to be prepared within 15 minutes of receipt and to be kept warm until picked up.

4. Nothing is to be prepared with a microwave oven.

5. Only noodles from the food plant are to be used in each item.

6. All health codes are to be met at all times.

7. Dishes and glassware are to be washed within five minutes of receipt and are to be spotless.

8. Sauce is to simmer a minimum of six hours.

9. A fresh fish will be offered every night.

10. All items are to be prepared on the premises with the exception of those items shipped from the food plant.

11. All beer and white wines are to be served chilled.

12. All items are to be properly garnished as to visual display standards.

13. All coffee is to be brewed fresh hourly. A brewed decaffeinated coffee is always to be available. Iced tea is to be brewed daily.

Part IV

Appendices

Appendix A

Strategic Planning Questionnaire for Organizational Assessment (Long Form)

Resource Availability in the Environment

1. Do we have good sources for employees?
2. Is our mix of hiring from the outside and promotion from within appropriate?
3. Do we have excessive dependency on a few suppliers?
4. Do we have good credit terms with suppliers?
5. Do our suppliers supply us with the proper mix of goods and services at the time and place and of the quality we need?
6. Do we have good lines of credit?
7. Is our debt-to-equity ratio appropriate?
8. Can we raise money easily in bond and equity markets?
9. Are we making use of available free information about our market (e.g., trade and professional literature and government studies)?
10. Do we hire consultants as needed and do they give us good information?

Source Inputs

1. Do our managers and employees have the proper mix of skills and abilities we need?
2. Do we encourage new ideas from our managers/employees?
3. Do our managers/employees have the proper physical characteristics to do the job?
4. Do we have a good racial, ethnic, and sex mixture of managers/employees?

5. Do our managers/employees have the proper interests and aptitudes to do their jobs?

6. Is the level of aspiration of our managers/employees high enough so that they are self-motivated?

7. Do our managers/employees have the proper tools and equipment to get the job done?

8. Do our managers and employees know expectations of performance?

9. Do we have capable purchasing agents who make good purchase decisions?

10. Are we energy efficient?

11. Do we have alternative sources of energy supply in case of shortages?

12. Is our transportation system efficient and effective at securing raw materials and semi-finished goods?

13. Is our plant and equipment outdated? (Is there a newer technology we should be using?)

14. Do we have enough of the proper type of land for future expansion?

15. Do we have idle plant, land, and equipment not generating a profit?

16. Are our unit budgets large enough to accomplish objectives?

17. Is there much waste in the way the budget is expended?

18. Are our budget and reporting procedures accurate and up to date?

19. Do we involve middle- and lower-level managers enough in budget determination?

20. Is our budget tied to objectives to be accomplished?

21. Are we using the right mix of stocks, bonds, loans, and retained earnings to finance growth?

22. Do we know enough about our customers and market?

23. Do we know our competition thoroughly?

24. Do we have a good human resource information system?

25. Does our legal staff keep us abreast of important legal developments?

26. Is our investment in new product research and development appropriate for future growth?

27. Do we know our market segments?

Management Functions and Decisions

1. Do we adequately forecast economic, demographic, technological, competitor, market, and social trends that could affect us?

2. Do we develop good goals on the basis of our forecasts?

3. Do we operationalize our goals and objectives by setting out clear paths for their achievement?

4. Are our goals measurable, specific, and realistic?

5. Are goals of various units integrated with one another and with overall organization goals?

6. Are our goals set in a participatory fashion and thus internalized by managers and employees?

7. Do we have clear-cut, realistic schedules for goal accomplishment?

8. Have we assigned goal accomplishment to specific people and units for accountability purposes?

9. Do we update our goals and schedules at least quarterly?

10. Do our managers/employees manage time efficiently?

11. Is our structure flexible or bureaucratic?

12. Have we properly pinpointed authority and accountability at all levels?

13. Do we have too many management levels?

14. Are our managers surrounded by too many staff assistants?

15. Are resources properly allocated to units and departments?

16. Are we recruiting the right types of managers and employees?

17. Do we have proper, unbiased selection techniques and procedures?

18. Do we hire the best people available for the salary?

19. Are our people placed in jobs commensurate with their training, experience, skills, abilities, and interests?

20. Are we abiding by all EEO regulations?

21. Do we have an accurate and up-to-date manpower plan?

22. Are we really committed to training and development for every employee?

23. Does every manager and employee have an agreed-upon career plan with the organization?

24. Are we willing to terminate unsatisfactory employees when necessary?

25. Are our wages and salaries at all levels competitive with the market?

26. Do we have a current personnel-policy manual?

27. Is our health and benefits system competitive within our industry and labor market?

28. Do we have a strong employee relations program?

29. If a union is not present, what are we legally doing to prevent a union from forming?

30. If a union is present, do we have a strong, constructive, and beneficial bargaining relationship?

31. Do we give our managers enough authority to make important decisions?

32. Do our managers practice an appropriate leadership style with their subordinates?

33. What is the quality of upward communication in our organization?

34. Is cross communication among departments good?

35. Are our memos, letters, and reports clear, concise, and to the point?

36. Are our meetings short and do they encourage constructive dialogue?

37. Do we provide a good incentive package to motivate employees?

38. Is merit rather than seniority our primary basis for pay raises and promotions?

39. Do our managers willingly coach and counsel problem employees?

40. Do we have a system of referral to professionals for problem employees?

41. How well do our reports help us monitor organization and unit performance?

42. Do we have an objectively based performance-appraisal system?

43. Is performance appraisal viewed as a joke around here?

44. Are our disciplinary procedures positive and corrective in nature, or are they punitive and negative?

45. Are we consistent and fair in our use of discipline?

46. Do we encourage feedback from our employees?

47. Is our face-to-face communication open, honest, and candid?

48. Do we have a good Management Information System that gives managers relevant, accurate information in just the right amount of detail on a timely basis?

Outputs

1. How successful are we in achieving organization-wide objectives?

2. How successful are we in achieving unit objectives?

3. Is our product/service mix current and competitive?

4. Do we generate enough profit to finance growth and to pay competitive dividends?

5. How satisfied are our employees?

6. How productive are our employees?

7. Does each unit have improvement as well as equilibrium objectives?

8. Does each manager and professional employee have personal (professional improvement) as well as unit and organization objectives?

9. Have we set proper priorities for our objectives?

10. Do we follow these priorities?

11. Do we do enough long-range planning and forecasting to set good long-range objectives?

12. Are our short-range, intermediate-range, and long-range objectives smoothly integrated?

13. Do we usually achieve our objectives within the time frames set?

Users in the Environment

1. Are our customers generally satisfied with our product/service offerings?
2. How loyal are our customers?
3. Why do people not buy our products or services?
4. Is our market share appropriate?
5. Do we have a good public image?
6. Is our advertising and promotion program viable?
7. Do we have an efficient and effective system for distribution of our products/services?
8. Do we have good government relations?
9. Do we have programs for employee families?
10. Do we provide a competitive rate of return on investment to our stockholders/owners?
11. Do we have a good stockholder-relations program?
12. Is our stock value/price appreciating at a good rate?

Monitoring and Feedback

1. Do we regularly monitor output for quality?
2. Do we regularly survey customers to ascertain levels of satisfaction?
3. Do we have good market research efforts that serve as the basis for new product/service development?
4. Can we effect changes in inputs and managerial decisions on the basis of information we gather on outputs and users?

Appendix B

Florida Power and Light Economic Forecast

This sample economic forecast is presented to demonstrate that an economic forecast need not be complex to be good. It embodies the essential aspects of an economic forecast and presents them in plain language for the reader. It is a valuable tool for the strategic plan.

CONTENTS

Economic Forecasts, 1984–1985   180

Summary   180

The National Economy   181

  Gross National Product   181
  Inflation Outlook   182
  Descriptions of Price Indexes   183

The Florida Economy   183

  Employment   185
  Manufacturing Employment   185
  Income   185
  Housing Industry   187

Alternative Economic Scenarios   187

LIST OF TABLES

1. Forecast of Real Gross National Product   184
2. Price Indexes, 1984–1994   184
3. Florida Economy   186
4. Ratio of Housing Starts for Each Year to Increase in Residential FPL Customers in December   188
5. CPI Forecast   189

6. Florida Non-Agricultural Employment   190
7. Florida Manufacturing Employment   191
8. Gross National Product   192
9. Florida Real Per Capita Income   193
10. Florida Real Total Personal Income   194
11. Florida Housing Starts   195
12. FPL Service Area Population Forecast   196
13. Florida Population Forecast   197
14. FPL Household Size Forecast   198

ECONOMIC FORECASTS, 1984–1985

The Energy Management Planning (EMP) Department's current economic forecast follows. For convenience and ease of presentation, the report is divided into three major sections: (1) the national economic forecast, (2) the economic forecast for the State of Florida, and (3) a set of economic scenarios.

It is important to note that, in preparing our economic forecast, we assumed that (1) there would be no major "supply shocks" or disruptions in the supply of essential raw materials, such as agricultural commodities or petroleum; (2) there would be no major international political disruptions that would have a significant impact on the U.S. economy; and (3) the Federal Reserve would attempt to keep the growth of monetary aggregates within their pre-determined "target" ranges. If any of these assumptions change, our forecast would change accordingly.

SUMMARY

The gross national product is expected to increase 6.6 percent in real terms for 1984. This growth rate is expected to moderate so that by 1985 the increase in real output will rise by 3.1 percent. Inflation, as measured by the consumer price index, is forecast to increase 5.0 percent in 1984 and rise to 6.0 percent in 1985.

Florida's economy will experience healthy growth in 1984 and a modest slowdown in that growth rate by 1985, paralleling the modest slowdown at the national level for the same period. Total non-agricultural employment is projected to grow 5.8 percent in 1984 and 5.3 percent in 1985. Real personal income is anticipated to rise by 6.0 percent in 1984 and by 4.0 percent in 1985.

The housing industry in Florida typically experiences very desultory growth rates throughout business cycles and the current period is no exception. Housing starts increased by 73 percent in 1983 over 1982. We are forecasting a 16 percent increase in 1984 and a 5 percent decrease in the growth rate in housing starts for 1985. This translates into 213,107 starts for 1984 and 202,452 starts for 1985, which is still high by recent comparisons. There is some evidence of overbuilding taking place, which is indicated by forming a ratio of new housing starts to the change in residential customers. A ratio of 1.0 suggests housing starts are keeping abreast of customer growth while a ratio of greater than 1.0 indicates starts are growing faster than residential customers; likewise, a ratio less than 1.0 suggests housing starts are not keeping apace of customer growth. The table of these ratios shows the ratios exceeding 1.0 for all seven standard Metropolitan Statistical Areas (SMSAs) in our service territory, which suggests some overbuilding is taking place in this industry.

THE NATIONAL ECONOMY

Gross National Product

The strong economic growth momentum that characterized 1983 is expected to carry over into 1984, making for a year of robust real GNP growth. This expectation has already come to fruition in 1984's first quarter, as indicated by the hefty 9.7 percent seasonally adjusted annual rate of growth in the nation's real gross national product. Most sectors of the nation's economy are expected to fare quite well this year. Rising personal incomes, increasing levels of employment, and increased business spending suggest that the current recovery will stay on track through the remainder of the year. However, the recent very high quarterly rates of growth in real gross national product cannot be sustained for a long period of time before the economy would move past its full employment equilibrium, rekindling inflationary pressures. Nevertheless, we in Florida Power & Light (FPL) forecasting expect real gross national product to grow by seasonally adjusted annual rates of 5.7 percent in 1984's second quarter, 3.5 percent during the third quarter, and 3.3 percent in 1984's final quarter. These quarterly rates of growth will result in a 6.6 percent year over year (1984 over 1983) increase in the nation's level of real gross national product for 1984.

The current recovery will be in its third year in 1985, and it is expected that the nation's economy will face some of the standard or typical problems associated with the latter (mature) stage of a business cycle expansion, such as a slowing in the rate of inventory accumulation, slower investment growth, and possibly some production bottlenecks. Consequently, real GNP growth is expected to slow in 1985. Although a recession is not envisioned for 1985, it is certainly a possibility, depending upon how high interest rates rise and the subsequent effects rising rates will have on interest sensitive sectors of the economy, such as housing, autos, durable goods, and business investment. However, our most probable forecast calls for a 3.1 percent growth (year over year) in 1985 for real GNP. This slowing down of the economy will carry over into 1986 when we expect real GNP to grow by 2.5 percent.

In the long run, the supply of factors of production, i.e., labor, capital, and raw materials (along with factor productivity increases), is more important in determining the growth of potential output of goods and services than is demand for these goods and services. Since the nation's labor force is expected to increase in the next 10 to 20 years by lower rates of growth than those rates recorded in the past two to three decades, total employment will also exhibit slower rates of growth. This suggests that real GNP can be expected to grow at lower rates than those rates experienced in the decades of the 1950s and 1960s, when employment growth was more robust. Also, the prospect of large federal budget deficits for the rest of this decade still looms on the horizon, threatening long-term economic growth. Because of these factors, we expect long-term annual real GNP growth to average about 3.0 percent per year, which is less than the 3.3 percent, 3.9 percent, and 3.1 percent compound average annual growth rates for real GNP that were posted in the decades of the 1950s, 1960s, and 1970s, respectively. However, the 3.0 percent average annual growth in real GNP that we envision for the 1987–1996 time period is greater than the 2.0 percent average annual rate of real GNP growth that was recorded for the last 10 years.

Inflation Outlook

Rates of price inflation have fallen dramatically in the past three to four years. Prices, as measured by the Consumer Price Index—All Urban Consumers (CPI-U), rose only 3.2 percent in 1983, which was the lowest rate of increase in over 15 years. Last year's 3.2 percent increase was significantly less than the 13.5 percent rate of increase in the CPI-U, which was recorded only three years earlier. Some, but not all, of the progress achieved in lowering the rate of inflation must be attributed to the severity of the most recent recession. However, other factors, such as (1) the Federal Reserve's emphasis on targeting money supply growth; (2) nationwide energy conservation efforts that have resulted in significantly lower rates of growth in the demand for energy consumption in the United States; and (3) deregulation of certain industries, have also played important roles in reducing inflation. Of course, in the post–World War II era, the first year of an economic recovery is usually characterized by a falling rate of inflation, and 1983 was no exception to this general pattern of price behavior.

The rate of inflation is expected to increase somewhat in 1984, as is typical in the second year of an economic recovery. Prices, as measured by the CPI-U, are forecast to increase by a rate of 5.0 percent in 1984.

A number of factors are expected to be at work in 1984, reducing the rate of inflation from what it might be otherwise. First of all, the beneficial effects of the deregulation of certain industries will promote competition and dampen price inflation. Secondly, the high value of the U.S. dollar on foreign exchange markets will lower the costs of imported goods to the United States, thereby forcing domestic producers (U.S. companies) to keep the prices of American-made goods in line. Also, the weakened position of many American labor unions, coupled with unemployment rates that are still high by historical standards, will tend to moderate wage and salary increases.

The rate of inflation, as measured by the CPI-U, is expected to reach 6.0 percent in 1985 and remain at that level throughout the remaining years of the forecast period. Although this is a relatively high rate of price increase when compared to the long-term historical trend, it is still considerably less than the 7.8 percent compound annual average rate of inflation that was recorded in the decade of the 1970s.

Reiterating, several factors, such as increased labor productivity, considerable price competition from imported goods, and the Federal Reserve's emphasis on controlling inflation by targeting the growth of monetary aggregates, will tend to keep inflation rates from reaching the high levels that were experienced in the 1970s and early 1980s.

Descriptions of Price Indexes

1. *Gross National Product Implicit Price Deflator.* The GNP deflator is the broadest price index that the EMP Department forecasts. The GNP deflator captures price trends for the four macro-economic sectors of the nation's economy, which are the household sector, the business sector, the government sector, and the foreign trade sector. The GNP deflator should be used where a very broad and comprehensive price measure is needed.

2. *Consumer Price Index—All Urban Consumers (CPI-U).* The Consumer Price Index is probably the best known and most often used price index that the EMP department forecasts. The CPI-U measures the price change, over time, of a given (constant) marketbasket of goods and services. The market basket consists of 382 goods and services (entry-level items) that represent the spending patterns of urban consumers. For FPL company purposes, the CPI-U is a useful escalator for determining trends in wage contracts and income payments. (An exception is hourly earnings in construction work. A separate index is provided for this category.)

3. *Producer Price Index—All Commodities (PPI).* The PPI (formerly the wholesale price index) is a comprehensive measure of the average changes in prices received in primary markets by producers of commodities in all stages of processing. This index represents price movements in the manufacturing, agricultural, forestry, fishing, mining, and public utilities sectors of the economy.

4. *Producer Price Index—Capital Equipment.* As a subset of the PPI for all commodities, the PPI capital equipment index measures changes in prices of capital equipment, such as trucks, generators, hand tools, machine tools, fans and blowers, and construction equipment.

5. *Average Hourly Earnings Index—Construction Workers.* This index reflects the changes in the average hourly earnings (wages) of construction workers.

THE FLORIDA ECONOMY

For the initial year of a recovery, Florida's economy was fairly vigorous in 1983. As is expected during the second year of a recovery, most of Florida's major economic variables are forecasted to grow at even faster rates this year. In fact, most measures of income and employment are forecasted to grow at their fastest rates since the late seventies.

At the same time, the rapid rates of economic growth achieved following the 1970–1971 and 1974–1975 recessions will not be repeated. The reasons for slower growth during this recovery are threefold. First, population growth, always an important stimulus to the Florida economy, is not expected to equal its

Table 1
Forecast of Real Gross National Product

Year	Billion 1972 Dollars	Percent Change From Previous Year
1984	1636.4	6.6
1985	1687.7	3.1
1986	1730.5	2.5
1987	1782.4	3.0
1988	1835.9	3.0
1989	1891.0	3.0
1990	1947.7	3.0
1991	2006.1	3.0
1992	2066.3	3.0
1993	2128.3	3.0
1994	2192.1	3.0
1995	2257.9	3.0
1996	2325.6	3.0

Table 2
Price Indexes 1984–1994

Year	GNP Deflator	% Change	Consumer Price Index	% Change	Producer Price Index: All commodities	% Change
1984	225.1	4.4	313.3	5.0	316.7	4.5
1985	237.7	5.6	332.1	6.0	334.1	5.5
1986	251.5	5.8	352.0	6.0	354.1	6.0
1987	266.3	5.9	373.1	6.0	375.7	6.1
1988–94	—	5.9 p.a.	—	6.0 p.a.	—	6.1 p.a.

Year	Producer Price Index Capital Equipment	% Change	Average Hourly Earnings Index: Construction Workers	% Change
1984	297.6	3.6	150.0	3.5
1985	314.0	5.5	158.3	5.5
1986	332.5	5.9	168.6	6.5
1987	352.8	6.1	180.6	7.1
1988–94	—	6.1 p.a.	—	7.1 p.a.

prior peaks. Second, as the Florida economy has matured, a number of local economies (Dade County is one notable example) have lost the ability to grow rapidly. Third, the most recent recession was less severe in Florida than was the recession experienced in 1974. It follows that lower rates of growth in employment and income are required during this recovery to re-employ those resources left idle during the recent recession. The specific forecasts that reflect these trends are discussed below.

Employment

Florida's total non-agricultural employment expanded by 3.0 percent during 1983. Employment in durable goods manufacturing and construction provided much of this growth. This year the recovery in services and trade, as well as manufacturing, should provide a strong base for employment growth. FPL is forecasting a 5.8 percent increase in total non-agricultural employment this year. This rate would tie with 1980 for the strongest employment growth in the last five years. The forecast assumes an average employment level of 4,094,420; up 224,120 from 1983's level.

The slower national recovery in the last half of 1984 is expected to suppress Florida's employment growth next year. A mild downturn in the housing industry should also hold down the rate of employment growth. During 1985, Florida's total non-agricultural employment is forecasted to increase 5.3 percent over this year's level. This would put Florida's total non-agricultural employment at 4,311,420.

Manufacturing Employment

The employment recovery thus far has been particularly strong in the manufacturing sector. Between December 1983 and March of this year the 12 month ending average of manufacturing employment jumped from an annual growth rate of 2.6 percent to 4.6 percent. This trend should continue through 1984 resulting in a 5.9 percent average annual increase in manufacturing employment. This forecast would place the level of manufacturing employment in 1984 at 499,500; up 27,800 from last year's level. By contrast, only half as many manufacturing employees were added in 1983.

As the pace of the national recovery moderates, manufacturing employment should slow to a 3.7 percent growth rate in 1985. Manufacturing as compared to total employment will experience a sharper reduction in its growth rate due to the sector's highly cyclical nature. The average level of manufacturing employment would be 518,000.

Income

An important measure of economic welfare is real per capita income, which is a gauge of the average purchasing power available to each Florida resident. In 1983, the state's real per capita income grew by 3.0 percent, a strong rebound from the prior year's 0.8 percent growth rate. With the continued strength of the state's recovery, real per capita income should increase by 4.0 percent this year.

Table 3
Florida Economy

	1984 (% Change)	1985 (% Change)
State		
Total Non-Agri. Employment	5.8	5.3
Manufacturing Employment	5.9	3.7
Housing Starts	16.0	−5.0
Real Personal Income	6.0	4.2
Real Per Capita	4.0	1.3
Brevard (Northeastern Division)		
Total Non-Agri. Employment	6.8	6.2
Manufacturing Employment	7.8	4.9
Housing Starts	20.0	−7.0
Broward (Southeastern Division)		
Total Non-Agri. Employment	6.0	5.5
Manufacturing Employment	5.9	3.7
Housing Starts	18.0	−10.0
Dade (Southern Division)		
Total Non-Agri. Employment	2.8	2.6
Manufacturing Employment	2.2	1.5
Housing Starts	15.0	−15.0
Lee (Western Division)		
Total Non-Agri. Employment	4.8	4.5
Manufacturing Employment	4.8	3.0
Housing Starts	7.5	0
Palm Beach (Eastern Division)		
Total Non-Agri. Employment	7.3	6.7
Manufacturing Employment	8.5	5.3
Housing Starts	25.0	0
Sarasota (Western Division)		
Total Non-Agri. Employment	6.8	6.2
Manufacturing Employment	6.5	4.7
Housing Starts	16.0	−5.0
Volusia (Northeastern Division)		
Total Non-Agri. Employment	4.4	4.0
Manufacturing Employment	6.8	4.1
Housing Starts	14.0	−5.0

This would put Florida's real per capita income at $4,040. In 1985, the pace of the national and state recoveries should moderate. At the same time, inflation is expected to accelerate. The result should be a slowdown in the growth of real per capita income. Thus, we expect a 1.3 percent rise in real per capita income next year.

Real personal income is determined by population and real per capita income. In 1983, Florida's total real personal income stood at $41,489,300; up 4.9 percent from 1982's level. With higher per capita income and a higher rate of population growth, real personal income should jump 6.0 percent this year. In 1985, population growth is expected to hold at this year's rate, while real per capita income drops to a slower growth rate. Accordingly, a 4.0 percent increase in Florida's real personal income in 1985 would be a reasonable estimate.

Housing Industry

Housing starts in 1983 increased at an explosive 73 percent growth rate. This exceptionally high rate of increase was due to a combination of three factors. First, the level of housing starts in 1982 was depressed. Second, the momentum of the rebound in housing starts had been building for several months due to an early recovery in that sector. Finally, interest rates dropped steadily through 1983.

This year circumstances are almost reversed. Last year's level of housing starts was high. The first quarter figures suggest that the momentum of the housing recovery is at a standstill. And, finally, the financial outlook is uncertain. Consequently, FPL is forecasting a slower rate of increase in the number of housing starts this year. According to our forecast, 213,107 housing starts will be built this year, a 16 percent increase over 1983's level. The number of housing starts is expected to drop 5 percent in 1985. The forecasted level of housing starts, 202,452, would still be high by historical standards.

Table 4 shows the ratio of housing starts to the increase in residential customers for the years 1974 to 1983. The data are for those counties that make up the major part of the five divisions' customers. A ratio of 1.0 suggests that housing starts are staying abreast of residential customer growth, while a ratio greater than 1.0 indicates that housing starts are accumulating faster than they can be absorbed. A ratio less than 1.0 suggests the potential for a "tight" housing market. It can be seen that for 1983 an "overbuild" condition seems imminent in these counties.

ALTERNATIVE ECONOMIC SCENARIOS

FPL's forecasting group has developed optimistic and pessimistic scenarios to accompany our standard economic forecast. While our forecast constitutes the most probable path the economy is likely to take, the scenarios consider possible deviations from that course. In considering deviations from the most probable case, the interdependencies among economic variables are maintained. Each scenario represents an alternative but consistent set of events.

The optimistic scenario is characterized by a higher-than-likely level of eco-

Table 4
Ratio of Housing Starts for Each Year to Increase in Residential FPL Customers in December

County	1983	1982	1981	1980	1979	1978	1977	1976	1975	1974
Brevard	1.08*	0.62	0.73	1.07	0.84	0.90	0.76	0.37	0.65	0.25
Broward	1.44	1.07	0.83	0.96	1.17	0.95	0.66	0.48	0.37	0.80
Dade*	2.04	1.25	1.75	1.04	1.34	0.77	0.75	0.77	1.07	1.22
Lee**	1.52	1.02	1.59	2.00	2.09	2.01	2.16	0.93	1.11	2.19
Palm Beach	1.43	0.82	1.00	1.06	1.43	1.09	1.08	0.73	0.47	0.55
Sarasota	1.06	0.68	1.02	1.07	0.89	0.86	0.78	0.60	0.57	1.53
Volusia**	1.63	1.75	1.57	1.43	1.67	1.34	0.87	0.77	0.85	0.82

*A ratio greater than 1.00 indicates more housing starts than added FPL customers.
**Other utilities serve many customers in these counties.

nomic activity. The national economy experiences a high rate of real GNP growth. At the same time, due to increases in productivity and the absence of any supply shocks, the rate of inflation is low. Contributing to this high rate of economic growth is a favorable business climate. A strong national economy encourages strong increases in Florida's population, employment, and income.

In the pessimistic scenario, economic activity is at a low level. The growth of real GNP is depressed. Supply shocks push up to the rate of inflation. Stagflation results. The effects on the Florida economy are low rates of population, income, and employment growth.

Because the scenarios are not linked to any explicit probabilities, they cannot be used as confidence intervals. Instead, the scenarios are provided as a recognition that contingencies may develop in the most probable forecast.

Table 5
CPI Forecast

Year	Low Value	Low % Change	Most Probable Value	Most Probable % Change	High Value	High % Change
1984			313.3	5.0		
1985	325.8	4.0	332.1	6.0	338.1	7.9
1986	338.9	4.0	352.0	6.0	368.5	9.0
1987	352.4	4.0	373.1	6.0	401.7	9.0
1988	366.5	4.0	395.5	6.0	437.4	9.0
1989	381.2	4.0	419.2	6.0	477.3	9.0
1990	396.4	4.0	444.4	6.0	520.3	9.0
1991	412.3	4.0	471.1	6.0	567.1	9.0
1992	428.8	4.0	499.4	6.0	618.1	9.0
1993	446.0	4.0	529.4	6.0	673.7	9.0
1994	463.8	4.0	561.2	6.0	734.3	9.0
1995	482.4	4.0	594.9	6.0	800.4	9.0
1996	501.7	4.0	630.6	6.0	872.4	9.0

	Compound Average Annual Growth Rate		
	Low	Most Probable	High
1984–94	4.0%	6.0%	8.9%

Table 6
Florida Non-Agricultural Employment (in thousands)

Year	Low Value	% Change	Most Probable Value	% Change	High Value	% Change
1984			4094.42	5.8		
1985	4196.78	2.5	4311.42	5.3	4426.6	8.1
1986	4268.13	1.7	4453.07	3.3.	4634.1	4.7
1987	4345.0	1.8	4581.5	2.9	4805.0	3.7
1988	4423.2	1.9	4713.0	2.9	4983.3	3.7
1989	4502.8	1.8	4848.3	2.9	5167.7	3.7
1990	4583.8	1.8	4987.6	2.9	5359.0	3.7
1991	4666.3	1.8	5130.5	2.9	5557.2	3.7
1992	4750.3	1.8	5277.8	2.9	5976.0	3.7
1993	4835.8	1.8	5429.3	2.9	6197.2	3.7
1994	4922.9	1.8	5585.0	2.9	6426.5	3.7
1995	5011.5	1.8	5745.4	2.9	6664.3	3.7
1996	5101.7	1.8	5910.7	2.9	6910.8	3.7

	Compound Average Annual Growth Rate		
	Low	Most Probable	High
1984–94	1.9%	3.2%	4.6%

Table 7
Florida Manufacturing Employment (in thousands)

Year	Low Value	Low % Change	Most Probable Value	Most Probable % Change	High Value	High % Change
1984			499.5	5.9		
1985	509.5	2.0	518.0	3.7	542.0	8.5
1986	514.1	0.9	533.5	3.0	568.0	4.8
1987	523.3	1.8	548.9	2.9	589.0	3.7
1988	532.7	1.8	564.8	2.9	610.8	3.7
1989	542.3	1.8	581.1	2.9	633.4	3.7
1990	552.1	1.8	597.9	2.9	656.8	3.7
1991	562.1	1.8	615.2	2.9	681.1	3.7
1992	572.2	1.8	632.9	2.9	706.3	3.7
1993	582.5	1.8	651.2	2.9	732.4	3.7
1994	593.0	1.8	670.0	2.9	759.6	3.7
1995	603.7	1.8	689.4	2.9	787.7	3.7
1996	614.5	1.8	709.3	2.9	816.8	3.7

	Compound Average Annual Growth Rate		
	Low	Most Probable	High
1984–94	1.7%	3.0%	4.3%

Table 8
Gross National Product (1972 dollars)

Year	Low Value	Low % Change	Most Probable Value	Most Probable % Change	High Value	High % Change
1984			1636.4	6.6		
1985	1639.2	1.0	1687.7	3.1	1696.0	4.5
1986	1652.3	0.8	1730.5	2.5	1757.1	3.6
1987	1668.9	1.0	1782.4	3.0	1836.2	4.5
1988	1685.6	1.0	1835.9	3.0	1818.8	4.5
1989	1702.4	1.0	1891.0	3.0	2005.1	4.5
1990	1719.4	1.0	1947.7	3.0	2095.4	4.5
1991	1736.6	1.0	2006.1	3.0	2189.7	4.5
1992	1754.0	1.0	2066.3	3.0	2288.2	4.5
1993	1771.5	1.0	2128.3	3.0	2391.2	4.5
1994	1789.3	1.0	2192.1	3.0	2498.8	4.5
1995	1807.1	1.0	2257.9	3.0	2611.2	4.5
1996	1825.2	1.0	2325.6	3.0	2728.7	4.5

	Compound Average Annual Growth Rate		
	Low	Most Probable	High
1984–94	1.0%	2.9%	4.4%

Table 9
Florida Real Per Capita Income (1967 dollars)

Year	Low		Most Probable		High	
	Value	% Change	Value	% Change	Value	% Change
1984			4,040			
1985	3,983	(1.4)	4,093	1.3	4,161	3.0
1986	3,948	(0.9)	4,167	1.8	4,299	3.3
1987	3,979	0.8	4,250	2.0	4,427	3.0
1988	4,011	0.8	4,335	2.0	4,529	2.3
1989	4,043	0.8	4,422	2.0	4,633	2.3
1990	4,104	1.5	4,510	2.0	4,740	2.3
1991	4,165	1.5	4,600	2.0	4,849	2.3
1992	4,228	1.5	4,692	2.0	4,961	2.3
1993	4,291	1.5	4,786	2.0	5,075	2.3
1994	4,356	1.5	4,882	2.0	5,191	2.3
1995	4,421	1.5	4,980	2.0	5,311	2.3
1996	4,487	1.5	5,080	2.0	5,433	2.3

	Compound Average Annual Growth Rate		
	Low	Most Probable	High
1984–94	0.8%	1.9%	2.5%

Table 10
Florida Real Total Personal Income (1967 dollars)

Year	Low Value	% Change	Most Probable Value	% Change	High Value	% Change
1984			43,995,600			
1985	43,995,600	0.0	45,825,228	4.2	46,943,305	6.7
1986	44,435,556	1.0	47,787,156	4.3	49,712,960	5.9
1987	45,413,138	2.2	49,924,750	4.1	52,298,034	5.2
1988	46,412,227	2.2	52,158,720	4.1	55,017,532	5.2
1989	47,433,296	2.2	54,501,150	4.1	57,878,443	5.2
1990	48,476,829	2.2	56,934,240	4.1	60,888,122	5.2
1991	49,543,319	2.2	59,146,800	4.1	64,054,304	5.2
1992	50,633,272	2.2	61,446,432	4.1	67,385,128	5.2
1993	51,747,204	2.2	63,840,454	4.1	70,889,155	5.2
1994	52,885,643	2.2	66,326,852	4.1	74,575,391	5.2
1995	54,049,127	2.2	68,913,240	4.1	78,453,311	5.2
1996	55,238,207	2.2	71,490,840	4.1	82,532,883	5.2

	Compound Average Annual Growth Rate		
	Low	Most Probable	High
1984–94	1.9%	4.2%	5.4%

Table 11
Florida Housing Starts (total for the year)

	Low		Most Probable		High	
	Value	% Change	Value	% Change	Value	% Change
1984			213,107	16.0		
1985	193,714		202,452	(5.0)	220,779	0.6
1986	184,029	(9.1)	210,550	4.0	240,649	9.0
1987	181,268	(5.0)	211,881	0.6	245,703	2.1
1988	178,549	(1.5)	213,221	0.6	250,862	2.1
1989	175,871	(1.5)	214,569	0.6	256,130	2.1
1990	173,233	(1.5)	215,925	0.6	261,509	2.1
1991	157,295	(9.2)	199,836	(7.5)	249,741	(4.5)
1992	142,824	(9.2)	184,945	(7.5)	238,503	(4.5)
1993	129,684	(9.2)	171,165	(7.5)	227,770	(4.5)
1994	117,753	(9.2)	158,411	(7.5)	217,521	(4.5)
1995	106,920	(9.2)	146,607	(7.5)	207,732	(4.5)
1996	97,083	(9.2)	135,683	(7.5)	198,384	(4.5)

	Compound Average Annual Growth Rate		
	Low	Most Probable	High
1984–94	(5.8%)	(2.9%)	0.2%

Table 12
FPL Service Area Population Forecast

Year	Low Value	Low % Change	Most Probable Value	Most Probable % Change	High Value	High % Change
1984			5,710,900			
1985	5,639,700	(1.2)	5,885,200	3.1	6,130,600	7.3
1986	5,735,300	1.7	6,038,700	2.6	6,340,300	3.4
1987	5,832,500	1.7	6,196,200	2.6	6,557,300	3.4
1988	5,931,400	1.7	6,357,800	2.6	6,781,600	3.4
1989	6,031,900	1.7	6,523,600	2.6	7,013,600	3.4
1990	6,134,200	1.7	6,693,700	2.6	7,253,600	3.4
1991	6,195,600	1.0	6,824,400	2.0	7,451,700	2.7
1992	6,257,600	1.0	6,957,700	2.0	7,655,100	2.7
1993	6,320,200	1.0	7,093,500	2.0	7,864,200	2.7
1994	6,383,500	1.0	7,232,100	2.0	8,078,900	2.7
1995	6,447,400	1.0	7,373,300	2.0	8,299,500	2.7
1996	6,499,700	0.8	7,506,900	1.8	8,512,100	2.6

	Compound Average Annual Growth Rate		
	Low	Most Probable	High
1984–94	1.1%	2.4%	3.5%

Source: University of Florida, Bureau of Economic and Business Research. *Population Studies*. Bulletin Number 68, April 1984.

Table 13
Florida Population Forecast

	Low		Most Probable		High	
	Value	**% Change**	**Value**	**% Change**	**Value**	**% Change**
1984			10,889,465	2.8		
1985	10,711,200	(1.6)	11,195,600	2.8	11,422,100	4.9
1986	10,897,600	1.7	11,467,700	2.4	11,739,100	2.8
1987	11,087,200	1.7	11,746,400	2.4	12,065,000	2.8
1988	11,280,100	1.7	12,031,900	2.4	12,399,900	2.8
1989	11,476,300	1.7	12,324,400	2.4	12,744,100	2.8
1990	11,676,000	1.7	12,623,900	2.4	13,097,800	2.8
1991	11,817,700	1.2	12,857,900	1.8	13,392,800	2.8
1992	11,961,100	1.2	13,096,300	1.8	13,694,400	2.3
1993	12,106,200	1.2	13,339,100	1.8	14,002,800	2.3
1994	12,253,100	1.2	13,586,300	1.8	14,318,100	2.3
1995	12,401,800	1.2	13,838,200	1.8	14,640,600	2.3
1996	12,543,700	1.1	14,072,900	1.7	14,936,900	2.0

	Compound Average Annual Growth Rate		
	Low	Most Probable	High
1984–94	1.2%	2.2%	2.8%

Source: University of Florida, Bureau of Economic and Business Research. *Population Studies*. Bulletin Number 68, April 1984.

Table 14
FPL Household Size Forecast

	Low		Most Probable		High	
	Value	% Change	Value	% Change	Value	% Change
1984			2.542			
1985	2.531	(0.4)	2.535	(0.3)	2.537	(0.2)
1986	2.506	(1.0)	2.517	(0.7)	2.527	(0.4)
1987	2.481	(1.0)	2.500	(0.7)	2.517	(0.4)
1988	2.456	(1.0)	2.482	(0.7)	2.507	(0.4)
1989	2.431	(1.0)	2.465	(0.7)	2.497	(0.4)
1990	2.414	(0.7)	2.450	(0.6)	2.487	(0.4)
1991	2.400	(0.6)	2.438	(0.5)	2.477	(0.4)
1992	2.388	(0.5)	2.428	(0.4)	2.469	(0.3)
1993	2.378	(0.4)	2.421	(0.3)	2.464	(0.2)
1994	2.371	(0.3)	2.416	(0.2)	2.464	0
1995	2.366	(0.2)	2.416	0	2.464	0
1996	2.366	0	2.416	0	2.464	0

	Compound Average Annual Growth Rate		
	Low	Most Probable	High
1984–94	(0.7)%	(0.5)%	(0.3)%

Bibliography

BOOKS AND JOURNAL ARTICLES ON STRATEGIC PLANNING

Amara, Roy. "Strategic Planning in a Changing Corporate Environment." *Long Range Planning,* February 1979, pp. 2–16.

> This paper concentrates on the fact that planning must, within a dynamic environment, be a learning process. The author develops a process cycle of planning, allocating, and monitoring strategic planning.

Amara, Roy C., and Andrew J. Lipinski. *Business Planning for an Uncertain Future.* Elmsford, N.Y.: Pergamon Press, 1983.

> Stressing that planning should be a line—not a staff—responsibility, the authors direct this book toward operating managers and line executives alike. They draw heavily on their experiences with over 100 of the Fortune 500 companies to combine current strategic management concepts with sophisticated forecasting methods.

Andersen, Theodore A. "Coordinating Strategic and Operational Planning." *Business Horizons,* Summer 1965, pp. 49–55.

> The coordination of all planning activities and goals is the subject of this classic article. Among the topics discussed are the aspects and differences between operational and strategic planning and methods for coordinating the plans.

Andrews, Kenneth R. "Corporate Strategy as a Vital Function of the Board." *Harvard Business Review,* November-December 1981, pp. 174–184.

> This article addresses the role of the board of directors in planning corporate strategy. The author also discusses strategic thinking in smaller companies and opposition to strategy committees.

Andrews, Kenneth R. "Directors' Responsibility for Corporate Strategy." *Harvard Business Review,* November-December 1980, pp. 30–42.

> The author answers the questions, "What is corporate strategy?" and "Why require corporate strategy?" and explores the directors' role in strategy development.

Andrews, Kenneth R. "Strategic Planning of Mice and Men." *Across the Board,* November 1983, pp. 6–9.
  This commentary explores the current state of strategic planning. Specifically, it addresses the current criticisms that some managers have made against formal long-term planning.

Ang, James S., and Jess H. Chua. "Long Range Planning in Large United States Corporations—A Survey." *Long Range Planning,* April 1979, pp. 99–102.
  The results of a survey of corporate planning in 500 large U.S. corporations form the basis of this article. Among the items discussed are the extent of long-range planning, the perceived benefits and problems of long-range planning, and the prevailing attitude toward long-range planning.

Ansoff, H. Igor. "Managing Strategic Surprise by Response to Weak Signals." *California Management Review,* Winter 1975, pp. 21–33.
  According to the author, strategic planning systems increasingly confront two difficulties: information about threats and opportunities is perceived too late to permit timely action; and the planning cycle is too long to permit timely response to fast-developing events. To combat these difficulties, the author introduces a technique for early identification of strategic signals and a real time planning system.

Argenti, John. "Corporate Planning and Corporate Collapse." *Long Range Planning,* December 1976, pp. 12–17.
  In this article, the author describes what he found during a year's investigation into company failure. He discusses the symptoms of failure and their implications for corporate planners.

Beck, P. W. "Corporate Planning for an Uncertain Future." *Long Range Planning,* August 1982, pp. 12–21.
  This article discusses the difficulties of planning in a complex socio-economic environment. Methods to help planners identify the forces behind changing circumstances are presented.

Bell, E. C. "Practical Long-Range Planning." *Business Horizons,* December 1968, pp. 45–49.
  With two case histories, the author illustrates the basic problems for all long-range planners—how to get a planning program accepted and used.

Bemelmans, T. "Strategic Planning for Research and Development." *Long Range Planning,* April 1979, pp. 33–44.
  This paper examines the need for and the difficulties in implementing strategies for planning the research and development activities of a company. A number of specific research strategies are outlined and related to strategic objectives.

Camillus, J. C. "Evaluating the Benefits of Formal Planning Systems." *Long Range Planning,* June 1975, pp. 33–40.
  The benefits that accrue from formalizing the planning process that cannot result from informal planning are the subject of this paper. The

author also discussed the inherent disadvantages that result from for-malization and the problems that can arise from faulty design.

Chambers, John C., et al. "How to Choose the Right Forecasting Technique." *Harvard Business Review,* July-August 1971, pp. 45–75.
This article discusses what every manager ought to know about the differ-ent kinds of forecasting and the times when they should be used. Included are charts that summarize the information presented.

Claxton, Christopher. "Planning Major International Projects." *Long Range Plan-ning,* April 1978, pp. 25–34.
This article primarily addresses engineering contracts, but its lessons can be extrapolated to other areas as well. Topics discussed include govern-ment involvement, financial considerations, and pricing considerations.

Cleland, David I., and William R. King. "Developing a Planning Culture for More Effective Strategic Planning." *Long Range Planning,* June 1974, pp. 70–74.
The authors of this article suggest that the success of long-range planning is less sensitive to the parameters of the planning techniques than it is to the overall culture in which the planning is accomplished. Therefore, they discuss the role of the chief executive and the planning staff, planning-related incentives, and other such topics.

Coley, John. *Corporate and Divisional Planning.* Reston, Va.: Reston Publishing Company, 1984.
This new text uses detailed case studies to demonstrate the interaction between divisions and corporate offices in diversified, decentralized com-panies and the complexities of setting unified goals and objectives in this environment. This book focuses not only on the planning process, but also the actual decisions that must be made.

Delombre, J., and B. Bruzelius. "Importance of Relative Market Share in Strate-gic Planning—A Case Study." *Long Range Planning,* August 1977, pp. 2–7.
This article addresses the relationship between market share and prof-itability and its implications for strategic planning. The product-portfolio approach and the product-line analysis are among the topics discussed.

Denning, Basil W. "Strategic Environmental Appraisal." *Long Range Planning,* March 1973, pp. 22–27.
This article provides a structure within which an executive can assess the effort being devoted to environmental appraisal and offers guidance in appraising the direction and scope of effort to obtain and select such information. Included is a list of sources of information for economic, technological, sociological, and political forecasts.

Derkinderen, Frans. "Pre-investment Planning." *Long Range Planning,* February 1977, pp. 2–8.
A strategic approach toward pre-planning of investments is developed in this article. Special attention is given to acceptance criteria, financing con-siderations, and types of commitment.

de Swart, J.M.M. "Personnel Planning—A Strategic View." *Long Range Planning*, June 1979, pp. 8–15.
> This article applies the strategic and operational planning process to personnel management. The author discusses the use and necessity of personnel planning, the personnel planning process, and the key problems of personnel planning.

Dyson, R. G., and M. J. Foster. "Making Planning More Effective." *Long Range Planning*, December 1983, pp. 68–73.
> A study of strategic planning in a set of 10 diverse organizations from both the public and private sector forms the content of this article. The authors discuss what constitutes effective planning and what impact participation has on that effectiveness.

Easterby-Smith, Mark, and Julia Davies. "Developing Strategic Thinking." *Long Range Planning*, August 1983, pp. 39–48.
> This paper addresses the problem of getting managers to contribute effectively to strategic planning. It provides a number of formal and less formal management development techniques for developing strategic awareness.

Eppink, D. Jan. "Planning for Strategic Flexibility." *Long Range Planning*, August 1978, pp. 9–15.
> According to this author, strategic flexibility is the tool needed to cope with increasing environmental uncertainty. In this article, the author explores the concept of flexibility and advances some implications on how to increase strategic flexibility.

Ernstthal, Henry L. "Ten Ways to Ensure Planning Failure." *Association Management*, December 1983, pp. 153–155.
> Ten recurring reasons for planning failure are identified and explained in this helpful article. The author also makes suggestions on how to avoid these common pitfalls.

Ford, T. Mitchell. "Strategic Planning—Myth or Reality? A Chief Executive's View." *Long Range Planning*, December 1981, pp. 9–11.
> The chairman, president, and chief executive officer of Emhart Corporation, the forty-first largest multinational in the United States, give their own personal views on strategic planning and make some practical suggestions.

Frohman, Alan L., and Domenic Bitondo. "Coordinating Business Strategy and Technical Planning." *Long Range Planning*, December 1981, pp. 58–67.
> Businesses that revolve around technology are the focus of this article. Among the topics discussed are identifying strategic technological issues and formulating the technological strategy.

Gerstner, Louis V. "Can Strategic Planning Pay Off?" *Business Horizons*, December 1972, pp. 5–16.
> This article takes a detailed look at the benefits and methods of strategic planning. Included are discussions of forecasting, top-down leadership, and performance appraisal.

Gilmore, Frank F., and Richard Brandenburg. "Anatomy of Corporate Planning." *Harvard Business Review*, November-December 1962, pp. 61–69.
The authors use a series of charts to provide a framework for discussing top-management planning problems and propose some solutions.

Glueck, William F., and Lawrence R. Jauch. *Business Policy and Strategic Management.* New York: McGraw-Hill Book Company, 1984.
This leading management text focuses on the relationship between business policy and strategic management. Over 30 cases demonstrate strategic management elements, strategic analysis, strategy formulation, and implementation and evaluation of strategic management.

Gotcher, J. William. "Strategic Planning in European Multinationals." *Long Range Planning*, October 1977, pp. 7–13.
This article summarizes a study of the effects of environmental changes on multinational business planning. Among the findings discussed are a shortening of time horizons and on increase in flexibility.

Hall, William K. "Forecasting Techniques for Use in the Corporate Planning Process." *Managerial Planning*, November/December 1972, pp. 5–10.
This article focuses upon the necessity for good forecasting procedures in corporate planning. Forecasting techniques discussed include the Delphi method, statistical models, and others.

Hall, William K. "The Impact of Managerial Behavior on Planning Effectiveness." *Managerial Planning*, September/October 1977, pp. 19–24.
The author suggests in this article that the way a manager manages an organization will have a bigger impact on planning effectiveness than the sophistication of the formal planning effort. As a result, he provides some guidelines by which managerial behavior can be directed to improve planning effectiveness.

Haner, F. T. "Risk Management in Corporate Planning." *Long Range Planning*, December 1981, pp. 12–16.
The use of a risk distribution matrix in corporate planning is the topic of this article. The author discusses how to get a comprehensive picture of the riskiness of the environment.

Harrigan, Kathryn Rudie. "Strategic Planning for Endgame." *Long Range Planning*, December 1982, pp. 45–48.
This article is based on the author's study of 61 firms managing businesses in environments of declining demand. Included are suggestions by which firms might better prepare for this problem.

Harrington, Diana R. "Stock Prices, Beta, and Strategic Planning." *Harvard Business Review*, May-June 1983, pp. 157–164.
The incorporation of a risk factor into strategic planning is the topic of this article. The actual problems of Alaska Interstate, Inc. are discussed.

Harrison, F. L. "How Corporate Planning Responds to Uncertainty." *Long Range Planning*, April 1976, pp. 88–93.
This article is based upon a research project into the influence of comput-

er methods on decision making. Topics covered include how managers cope with planning in conditions of extreme uncertainty about future economic and business conditions and how the role of strategic planning is changing.

Hershey, Robert. "Planning for the Unthinkable." *Harvard Business Review.* July-August 1975, pp. 20–24.
The author suggests in this article that most events that arise can be anticipated, and he offers methods to plan for both natural and man-made disasters.

Higgins, Richard B. "Reunite Management and Planning." *Long Range Planning,* August 1976, pp. 40–45.
The reunion of planning and decision-making executives is the focus of this paper. The author describes how planning activities can be returned to the mainstream of organizational life.

Hobbs, John M., and Donald F. Heany. "Coupling Strategy to Operating Plans." *Harvard Business Review.* May-June 1977, pp. 119–126.
The authors of this article discuss the gap between the authors of strategic plans and those who prepare operating plans. Among the topics discussed are the reasons for this gap, the problems it causes, and the methods to close it.

Hofer, Charles W. and Dan Schendel. *Strategy Formulation: Analytical Concepts.* St. Paul, Minn.: West Publ. Co., 1978.
Presents a comprehensive approach to analyzing overall corporate strategy as well as specific strategies in individual business lines.

Holmberg, Steven R. "Monitoring Long-Range Plans." *Long Range Planning,* June 1974, pp. 63–69.
The results of a survey of U.S. utility firms provide insights into the monitoring phase of long-range planning in this article. The author measures plans versus results for a number of items including marketing, plant and equipment, and research and development.

Howlett, Michael J. "Strategic Planning in State Government." *Managerial Planning,* November/December 1975, pp. 10–16.
The application of strategic business planning to state government is described in this article by the former secretary of the State of Illinois. He includes a discussion of organizational missions, objectives, and program statements.

Karger, Delmar, and Zafar Malik. "Long Range Planning and Organizational Performance." *Long Range Planning,* December 1975, pp. 60–64.
This article summarizes a study undertaken to measure the effects of long-range planning upon commonly accepted financial performance measures in industrial firms. Industries discussed are chemical and drugs, electronics, and machinery.

Kloeze, H. J., et al. "Strategic Planning and Participation: A Contradiction in Terms." *Long Range Planning,* October 1980, pp. 10–20.

This article deals with internal participation in strategic planning. The authors present an organizational framework that will maintain flexibility and alertness and ensure that planning is controlled and managed.

Koontz, Harold. "Making Strategic Planning Work." *Business Horizons,* April 1976, pp. 37–47.
The author gives guidelines for effective implementation of strategic planning in this helpful article. Discussed are the major types of strategy, strategy requisites, and many other important topics.

Kotov, Fyodor. "Long-Term Planning in the U.S.S.R." *Long Range Planning,* August 1975, pp. 61–63.
The author, a deputy head of the U.S.S.R. state planning committee, illustrates the approach to long-term planning used by centrally planned economies. This is an interesting, informative, and useful look at long-term planning.

Krijnen, Hans G. "Formulating Corporate Objectives and Strategies." *Long Range Planning,* August 1977, pp. 78–87.
In this article, the author uses three economic objectives and three groups of strategies to illustrate part of the strategic policy-making of a firm. He then develops some broad guidelines from the relationships discussed.

Kudla, Ronald J. "The Effects of Strategic Planning on Common Stock Returns." *Academy of Management Journal,* March 1980, pp. 5–21.
The purpose of this article was to explore the economic effects of strategic planning on financial performance as measured by stockholder returns. The results of a survey of the Fortune 500 and 57 other firms are discussed in the article.

Kudla, Ronald J. "Elements of Effective Corporate Planning." *Long Range Planning,* August 1976, pp. 82–93.
Interviews with 14 corporate planning executives provided the input for this paper. Areas focused upon include preceptions of a need for planning, analysis of planning and organizational structure, and elements of effective planning.

La Forge, Lawrence, and D. Robley Wood. "Corporate Planning and Operations Research: Do They Go Together?" *Long Range Planning,* June 1982, pp. 152–156.
A survey of corporate planners in 59 U.S. commercial banks led to this article on the relationship between operations research activities and corporate planning. Included in the survey results is a financial comparison between operations research users and non-users.

Leontiades, Milton. "The Dimensions of Planning in Large, Industrialized Organizations." *California Management Review,* Summer 1980, pp. 82–86.
A survey of chief executive officers and planning officers provided the basis for this paper. The author discusses the evolution of planning systems and the use of non-traditional planning, among other subjects.

Martin, John. "Business Planning: The Gap between Theory and Practice." *Long Range Planning,* December 1979, pp. 2–10.

The gap between corporate planning advocated by theorists and actual planning systems of large corporations is examined in this paper. The author explores both formal and informal planning.

Michael, Stephen R. "Tailor-Made Planning: Making the Planning Fit the Firm." *Long Range Planning,* December 1980, pp. 74–79.
This article demonstrates a limited application of the contingency approach to planning, which is intended to show that the process is highly flexible and can be adapted to the organization's requirements.

Mintzberg, Henry. "Planning on the Left Side and Managing on the Right." *Harvard Business Review,* July-August 1976, pp. 49–58.
This article addresses the differences in the two hemispheres of the human brain and the implications of those differences to the manager. An interesting look at the analytic and intuitive minds.

Moyer, Reed. "The Futility of Forecasting." *Long Range Planning,* February 1984, pp. 65–72.
According to the author, long-range forecasting is an integral part of planning, but relying on its accuracy may be a mistake. This article studies performances of some forecasts, analyzes factors contributing to forecast error, and suggests ways in which management may deal with the uncertainty resulting from faulty forecasting performances.

Murakami, Teruyasu. "Recent Changes in Long Range Corporate Planning in Japan." *Long Range Planning,* April 1978, pp. 2–5.
A new stage in Japanese long-range corporate planning that resulted from a difficult economic situation provides the basis for this article. Included is a discussion of the long-range plans of Hitachi.

Naylor, Thomas N. "How to Integrate Strategic Planning into Your Management Process." *Long Range Planning,* October 1981, pp. 56–61.
This article defines some of the problems involved in integrating strategic planning and strategic-planning tools into the decision process and suggests some possible solutions to these problems.

Naylor, Thomas N., and Daniel R. Gattis. "Corporate Planning Models." *California Management Review,* Summer 1976, pp. 69–78.
The results of a survey of almost 2,000 firms in the United States, Canada, and Europe provide the basis for this article. Topics covered include how planning is used, who receives the planning output, and what forecasting techniques are used.

Newgren, Kenneth E., and Archie B. Carroll. "Social Forecasting in U.S. Corporations—A Survey." *Long Range Planning,* August 1979, pp. 59–64.
A survey into firms' social responsiveness as a function of the state of the economy provides the basis for this article. The authors specifically address the relationship between social forecasting and strategic planning.

Newman, William H. "Shaping the Master Strategy of Your Firm." *California Management Review,* Spring 1967, pp. 77–88.
This classic article addresses the means by which master strategy can deal

with elements of change, growth, and adaptation. Included are discussions of supply and demand, industry climate, market position, and many other crucial factors.

Paul, Ronald N., et al. "The Reality Gap in Strategic Planning." *Harvard Business Review*, May-June 1978, pp. 124–130.
In this article, the authors identify the two basic problems inherent in planning—producing reasonably accurate forecasts and misusing the strategic plan as an operating document—and propose ways for companies to overcome these problems.

Pearson, Barrie. "A Business Development Approach to Planning." *Long Range Planning*, December 1976, pp. 54–62.
In this article, the author promotes the idea that planning takes a project-oriented rather than procedure-oriented approach. Included is a discussion of the roles of business development executives.

Pennington, Malcolm W. "Why Has Planning Failed?" *Long Range Planning*, March 1972, pp. 2–9.
The author of this article suggests that planning is not making as important a contribution to corporate accomplishment as it should, and suggests reasons why this is true. He also provides helpful rules that include involving top management only at key points, not to look for a perfect answer, and involving doers in the planning.

Peters, Thomas J. and Robert H. Waterman. *In Search of Excellence.* New York: Harper & Row, 1982.
A best-seller which describes lessons to be learned from the nation's best run companies.

Porter, Michael E. *Competitive Strategy.* New York: The Free Press, 1980.
This wide selling book describes techniques for analyzing industries and competitors.

Reed, Stanley Foster. "Corporate Growth by Strategic Planning, Part I: Developing a Strategy." *Mergers and Acquisitions,* Summer 1977, pp. 4–13. "Corporate Growth by Strategic Planning, Part II: Developing a Plan." *Mergers and Acquisitions,* Fall 1977, pp. 4–27. "Corporate Growth by Strategic Planning, Part III: Developing a Methodology." *Mergers and Acquisitions,* Winter 1978, pp. 19–37.
In this three-part series, the editor and publisher of *Mergers and Acquisitions* presents a new approach to corporate diversification. Among the numerous topics discussed is an informative section on the importance of corporate strategy.

Reimnitz, Charles A. "Testing a Planning and Control Model in Nonprofit Organizations." *Academy of Management Journal,* March 1972, pp. 77–90.
This article discusses a study that utilized a general planning model to test the relative efficiency of administrators in three educational service organizations. Included is a discussion of the areas that affect managerial proficiency.

Ringbakk, Kjell-Arne. "Strategic Planning in a Turbulent International Environment." *Long Range Planning,* June 1976, pp. 2–11.

Changing environments, changing host country demands, and changing attitudes toward multinational corporations are the subjects of this article. The author addresses these issues and their implications for multinational corporate strategic planning.

Roney, C. W. "How to Accomplish the Two Purposes of Business Planning." *Managerial Planning*, January/February 1977, pp. 1–11.
This article defines two purposes of planning—protective and affirmative—and suggests ways to accomplish these purposes. Included is a six-step procedure for successful planning.

Ruffat, Jean. "Strategic Management of Public and Non-market Corporations." *Long Range Planning*, April 1983, pp. 74–84.
In this article, the author develops a strategic framework for the management of public companies. Much attention is given to the companies' socio-economic environments.

Rumelt, Richard. *Strategy, Structure, and Economic Performance*. Cambridge, Mass.: Harvard University Press, 1974.
Strategy is related to organization structure and to economic performance. Various strategies and their relationships to structure and performance are depicted.

Saunders, Charles B. and Francis D. Tuggle. "Why Planners Don't." *Long Range Planning*, June 1977, pp. 19–24.
A study of the planning function in five major U.S. corporations, none of which engaged in true strategic planning, led to this article. The authors discuss why planners don't plan based on environmental, organizational, and managerial characteristics of the firms.

Schmidt, Richard F. "Strategic Planning: Off-Limits for Financial Managers?" *Management Review*, June 1979, pp. 7–12.
This article addresses the application of strategic planning to financial management and the differences between strategic planning and budgeting. Included is a section on how a financial manager can contribute to the strategic plan.

Schoeffler, Sidney, et al. "Impact of Strategic Planning on Profit Performance." *Harvard Business Review*, March-April 1974, pp. 137–145.
The highlights of the Marketing Science Institute's study on the profit impact of market strategies is the topic of this article. The authors discuss the profit performances of different types of businesses under different competitive conditions.

Shanklin, William L. "Strategic Business Planning: Yesterday, Today, and Tomorrow." *Business Horizons*, October 1979, pp. 7–14.
This article examines the changes in business planning strategies from the 1960s to 1980. It discusses corporate growth in the 1960s and 1970s and makes predictions for the 1980s.

Smith, G. "Planning for Productivity." *Long Range Planning*, April 1980, pp. 52–59.

According to the author, the need to improve productivity and business performance is urgent, yet it is neglected. This article tells how to plan for increased productivity.

Snyder, Neil, and William F. Glueck. "How Managers Plan—The Analysis of Managers' Activities." *Long Range Planning,* February 1980, pp. 70–76.
This paper analyzes the positions of Mintzberg and planning experts on the extent to which managers plan and the importance of planning to management. While Mintzberg contends that managers do not plan, the authors' findings suggest otherwise.

Steiner, George A. "Approaches to Long-Range Planning for Small Business." *California Management Review,* Fall 1967, pp. 3–16.
The application of long-range planning techniques to small business is the focus of this classic article. Break-even analysis and return on investment are among the topics discussed.

Steiner, George A., et al. "Formal Strategic Planning in the United States Today." *Long Range Planning,* June 1983, pp. 12–17.
In this article, the author gives an appraisal of the state of corporate strategic planning in the United States. He utilizes a set of criteria that may be used by individuals and companies to assess their own planning systems.

Steiner, George A.; John B. Miner; and Edmund R. Gray. *Management Policy and Strategy.* New York: Macmillan Publishing Company, 1982.
This well-respected text includes 18 chapters and numerous cases used to demonstrate the nature of business strategy, the formulation of business strategy, the implementation of business strategy, and many other topics.

Steiner, George A. and Hans Schollhammer. "Pitfalls in Multinational Long-Range Planning." *Long Range Planning,* April 1975, pp. 2–12.
The authors of this article discuss the major pitfalls which should be avoided to ensure effective long-range planning. Also included are the least important pitfalls.

Stotland, Jack A. "Planning Acquisitions and Mergers." *Long Range Planning,* February 1976, pp. 66–71.
This article explores the steps a company should take from the time it decides to expand by acquisition to the time the acquisition is integrated into the firm. Included are discussions of an internal audit, an acquisition search, and a negotiation and re-evaluation.

Taylor, Bernard. "New Dimensions in Corporate Planning." *Long Range Planning,* December 1976, pp. 80–106.
This article compares and contrasts five different and complementary views of planning. It addresses planning as a control system, as a framework for innovation, as a social learning process, as a political process, and as a conflict of values.

Taylor, Bernard. "Strategic Planning for Social and Political Change." *Long Range Planning,* February 1974, pp. 33–39.

In this article, the author points out the necessity of assessing social and political challenges to the corporation, and describes how to formulate and implement social and political plans aimed to ensure the company's survival. Included are examples of the major crises large companies have faced.

Taylor, Ronald N. "Psychological Aspects of Planning." *Long Range Planning,* April 1976, pp. 66–74.
This article examines the impact of perceptual processes, cognitive ability, motivation, and values on corporate planning. Topics discussed include resistance to planning, cognitive limitations in implementing plans, and blocks to innovative planning.

Terry, P. T. "Mechanisms for Environmental Scanning." *Long Range Planning,* June 1977, pp. 2–9.
This article describes some of the mechanisms that have been used to help companies scan their environments as a part of planning and controlling in a turbulent environment. Topics discussed include market influences, technical influences, social influences, and political influences.

Thomas, Philip S. "Environmental Scanning—The State of the Art." *Long Range Planning,* February 1980, pp. 20–25.
In this article, the author provides evidence of nine leading organizations in which the practice of scanning for planning is effectively used. He describes both the purposes and processes of effective environmental scanning.

Thune, Stanley S., and Robert House. "Where Long-Range Planning Pays Off." *Business Horizons,* August 1970, pp. 81–87.
The findings of the authors' study of firms in six industrial groups form the content of this article. They discuss the effects of formal and informal planning in the drug, chemical, machinery, food, oil, and steel industries.

Thurston, Philip H. "Should Smaller Companies Make Formal Plans?" *Harvard Business Review,* September-October 1983, pp. 162–188.
In this article, the author discusses the various factors that must be assessed to determine the proper planning approach for smaller companies. The disadvantages of formal planning processes are also discussed.

Tichey, Noel M. *Managing Strategic Change.* New York: John Wiley and Sons, 1983.
This management text focuses on three important aspects of any change process: the technical, political, and cultural components. It also suggests strategies for dealing effectively with these components.

Tipgos, Manuel A. "Structuring a Management Information System for Strategic Planning." *Managerial Planning,* January/February 1975, pp. 10–16.
This article addresses the nature and scope of strategic planning and information systems. Topics discussed include such items as information requirements and storage requirements.

Turner, Robert C. "Should You Take Business Forecasting Seriously?" *Business Horizons,* April 1978, pp. 64–72.

    Business forecasting is an important part of strategic planning, and its role is examined in this useful article. Included are discussions of internal and external influences, changing economic relationships, and sources of error.

Unni, V. K. "The Role of Strategic Planning in Small Businesses." *Long Range Planning,* April 1981, pp. 54–58.

    A survey of 110 small businesses provided the input for this paper. The author describes the role of judgment, experience, and intuition in small business planning.

Vesper, Volker D. "Strategic Mapping—A Tool for Corporate Planners." *Long Range Planning,* December 1979, pp. 75–93.

    This article summarizes the management concept of strategic mapping. Included is a complete discussion of the matrix technique and a set of seven executive strategy guidelines.

von Lanzenaver, Christopher, and Michael R. Sprung. "Developing Inflation Scenarios." *Long Range Planning,* August 1982, pp. 37–44.

    This article describes a scenario-based approach of forecasting future levels of inflation. The method used was developed for retirement income planning.

Welch, Jonathan B. "Strategic Planning Could Improve Your Share Price." *Long Range Planning,* April 1984, pp. 144–147.

    This article addresses the financial results of strategic planning. Specifically, the results of a study to determine if and how strategic planning affects the price-earnings multiple are presented.

Wheelen, Thomas L., and J. David Hunger. *Strategic Management and Business Policy.* Reading, Mass.: Addison-Wesley Publishing Company, 1983.

    This text is recognized as a leading book on strategic management. It includes 11 chapters and 36 cases dealing with corporate strategy, environmental issues, boards of directors, multinational strategy, and not-for-profit strategy.

Wheelwright, Steven C., and Robert L. Banks. "Involving Operating Managers in Planning Process Evolution." *Sloan Management Review,* Summer 1979, pp. 43–59.

    In this study of six companies, the authors indicate the importance of viewing the development of planning systems as an evolutionary process. Specific attention is focused on how operating managers can be involved at each stage of the planning process evolution to improve the fit between long- and short-term goals.

Wilson, Ian H., et al. "Strategic Planning for Marketers." *Business Horizons,* December 1978, pp. 65–73.

    The application of strategic planning to marketing forms the basis for this article. Strategic planning at General Electric is one of the topics discussed.

Wood, D. Robley Jr., and R. Lawrence LaForge. "The Impact of Comprehensive Planning on Financial Performance." *Academy of Management Journal,* pp. 516–526.
  This article explains the results of a survey of large U.S. banks that examined the relationship between formal planning procedures and financial performance.

Wrapp, H. Edward. "Organization for Long-Range Planning." *Harvard Business Review,* January-February 1957, pp. 37–47.
  This classic article explores the means and methods of effective organization for successful long-range planning. The author discusses the roles of operating managers, vice-presidents, divisional heads, and specialists and consultants, along with a host of other topics.

Index

Action planning. *See* Action steps
Action steps, 97–122; completeness achieving, 98; concurrency issue, 100; decision tree analysis, 100, 101; determining, 97–98; development of, 97–100; using objectives, 98; personnel involvement, 97; sample, 98; scenario building, 100; Spina's Fine Foods, Inc., 160–61, 163; tie-in sheets, 112–15. *See also* Action steps scheduling; Contingency planning
Action steps scheduling, 100, 102–4; computer use, 108; optimistic-pessimistic scheduling, 103–4; paperwork minimizing, 108, 109; personnel involvement, 100; realistic time, 103; slack time, 103. *See also* End-point scheduling; Time management; *specific tools*
Add-on budgeting, 124
Analysis paralysis, 61

Bar chart, 105; sample, 105; worksheet, 107
Boston Consulting Group, product/service analysis model, 66, 69–70
Budget, 123–127; add-on budgeting, 124; budget integrity, 124; incremental budgeting, 124; Program

Planning Budgeting System (PPBS), 125; reasons for, 123–124; Spina's Fine Foods, Inc., 163, 165, 166; zero-based budgeting, 124–127
Business Week, strategic planning article, 13

Calendars, 104–5; color-coding, 104, 105; desk-top, 104; loose-leaf notebook system, 105; pocket, 105; tickler file, 104; wall, 105
Committees for strategic planning, 16
Computers: use in action steps scheduling, 108; use in scenarios, 59; use in tracking system, 128–29
Contingency planning, 99–100; plans development, 99; probability analysis, 99; sample plans, 99–100
Corrective action systems, 132–43; definition, 132; equipment performance, 133; management directive, 135; objectives/goals performance, 133–34; personnel audit, 135–36; personnel performance, 132–33; plans failing list, 137–39; policy audit, 135; sample, 136–37, 138; self-correcting, 135–36, 139; for tracking system, 132; worksheet, 136–37. *See also* Corrective action systems characteristics; Problem solving

Corrective action systems characteristics, 134; future orientation,
134; positive, 134; preventive, 134;
timeliness, 134

Customer/Market analysis, 4, 49–57;
consumer definition, 49; customer
definition, 49–50; customer driven
factor, 50; Spina's Fine Foods, Inc.,
154. *See also* Customer profile;
Market·growth projection; Market
research

Customer profile, 50–51, 52–53;
change, 50–51; demographic, 50;
projected growth, 51, 54; psychological, 50; Spina's Fine Foods,
Inc., 155

Decision tree analysis, 100, 101

Delphi Method: use in environmental
forecast, 48; use in objectives developing, 87; use in objectives prioritizing, 95

End-point scheduling, 102–3; step
delegating, 103; step listing, 102;
step postponing, 103; step prioritizing, 102–3; time estimating,
102. *See also* Action steps
scheduling

Environmental analysis, 4, 25–40;
boundary-spanning units, 34, 36–
37; domain, 28; domain concensus,
28; environmental assessment, 33–
34; environmental constraints, 31–
32, 37; environmental opportunities, 31, 37; environmental
scanning, 25–26, 42; nonrelevant
environment, 28; use in objectives
prioritizing, 94; outside environment scoping, 27; potentially relevant environment, 28; relevant
environment, 26; Spina's Fine
Foods, Inc., 150–51; workshop
form, 35–36. *See also* Environmental sectors; Issues analysis method

Environmental forecast, 4, 41–48;
construction of, 41–42; Delphi
Method, 48; environmental scan-

ning, 42; environmental sectors,
42; information quantifying, 42,
44, 46; nominal group training
(NGT), 47–48; use in objectives
prioritizing, 94; sample forecast,
45–46; Spina's Fine Foods, Inc.,
151–54; use in strategic planning
premises, 58; trend line analysis,
41, 46–47; worksheet, 43–44

Environmental sectors: competition,
29; demographics, 29–30; distributors, 30; economy, 29; energy
supplies, 31; use in environmental
forecast, 42; international conditions, 31; labor market, 30;
legal/political ramifications, 29;
physical resources, 30; societal values, 29; suppliers, 30; technology,
30; transportation, 31

Focus groups: use in internal assessment, 65; use in market research,
56

Gantt chart, 105; sample, 106;
Spina's Fine Foods, Inc., 162;
worksheet, 107

Goals. *See* Strategic thrusts

Group facilitator, 17, 63, 87–88

Implementing. *See* Action steps

Incremental budgeting, 124

Internal assessment, 4, 62–74; data
gathering methods, 65–66; essay
form, 65; financial analysis, 70–74;
financial statement sample, 73;
focus groups, 65; interviews, 65;
use in objectives prioritizing, 94;
organization factors, 63, 64; problem identifying, 62–63, 65; problem solving worksheet, 140–41;
product/service analysis, 66, 69–
70; questionnaires, 65–66, 173–
177; role model, 62–63; Spina's
Fine Foods, Inc., 156, 157–58;
strengths/weaknesses identification,
62, 64; Survey Feedback Instrument, 65, 66, 67–68; workshops,
63. *See also* Ratios

Issues analysis method, 37–40; constituent interest correlation workshop form, 38; Issues Alert System Matrix workshop form, 39

Line/staff conflict, 14; minimizing, 14, 15–16
Line/staff relationships, 15

Management audit. *See* Internal assessment
Management by objectives (MBO), 6 10
Management review. *See* Internal assessment
Market analysis. *See* Customer/Market analysis
Market growth projection, 51, 53, 54; by adding markets, 51, 54; company growth philosophy, 54; competitor markets growth, 51; economic conditions, 54; existing markets growth, 51; managing growth, 54; population trends, 51, 54; sales growth, 51; Spina's Fine Foods, Inc., 156; state of technology, 54
Market research, 54–57; census data, 55; consultants, 55; consumer complaints, 56; consumer panels, 56; customer observation, 56–57; dealer feedback, 56; employee suggestions, 56; focus groups, 56; in-house department, 55; public information, 55; salesforce feedback, 56; warranty registration information, 56
Measuring system. *See* Tracking system characteristics
Mission development. *See* Mission statement
Mission statement, 6, 75–78; use in objectives prioritizing, 94–95; sample statements, 77; worksheet, 78. *See also* Mission statement key elements
Mission statement key elements, 76, 78; brevity, 76; consistency, 78; economic efficiency, 76; market,

76; organization distinction, 76; organization purpose, 76; products/services, 76; time frame, 76; understandability, 78
Monitoring system. *See* tracking system characteristics

Nominal group training (NGT): use in environmental forecast, 47–48; use in objectives developing, 87; use in objectives prioritizing, 95

Objectives developing, 85–96; in action steps, 98; autocratic announcement, 85–86; concensus participation, 86; consultive method, 86; Delphi Method, 87; democratic participation, 86; free reign participation, 86–87; group facilitator, 87–88; nominal group training, 87; objectives criteria, 88, 89; objectives quantifying, 88, 89; objectives rationale, 88; participative approaches, 86–87; use of strategic thrusts, 85, 90–91; using tie-in sheets, 111–13, 114–15; time frame, 93; writing objectives worksheet, 92; workshop, 87. *See also* Budget; Objectives prioritizing; Objectives types
Objectives prioritizing, 94–96; Delphi Method, 95; use of environmental analysis, 94; use of environmental forecast, 94; use of internal assessment, 94; use of mission statement, 94–95; nominal group training, 95; paired comparison technique, 95–96; relate to problems/opportunities, 94; rank ordering, 95; use of strategic thrusts, 94
Objectives types, 92–94; career development, 93; equilibrium, 93; improvement, 92–94; organizational units, 93–94
Operations analysis. *See* Internal assessment
Optimistic-pessimistic scheduling, 103–4

Organizational assessment. *See* Internal assessment

Organization audit. *See* Internal assessment

Personnel: action steps involvement, 97, 100; audit of, 135–36; performance, 132–33; strategic planning involvement, 12–14

PERT (Program Evaluation Review Technique) chart, 105, 108; color-coding, 108; critical path (CP), 108; sample, 108, 109; Spina's Fine Foods, Inc., 164

Planning horizon, 22–23

Planning process. *See* Strategic planning process

Plan operationalizing, 6, 83, 85, 86. *See also specific elements of*

Problem solving, 139–43; in internal assessment, 140–41; probing, 140; problem defining, 140; symptom treating, 139–40; worksheet, 140–41. *See also* Corrective action systems

Product/Service analysis, 66, 69–70; cash cows, 69; dogs, 70; matrix worksheet, 69; question marks, 70; stars, 69

Programming. *See* Action steps

Program Planning Budgeting System (PPBS), 125

Quality circle, 65

Ratios, 70–74; acid, 71; activity, 71; average collection period, 71; coverage, 73; current, 71; debt, 71; debt-to-equity, 72–73; financial statement sample, 73; fixed charge coverage, 73; guidelines for use, 74; inventory turnover, 71; leverage, 71; liquidity, 71; profitability, 74; profit margin on sales, 74; quick, 71; ratio comparisons, 70; return on assets, 74; return on net worth, 74; summary sheet, 72;

times interest earned, 73; total asset turnover, 71

Realistic time, 103

Scenarios, 58–59; in action steps, 100; computer use, 59; in strategic planning premises, 58–59

Scheduling. *See specific types*

Scheduling tools. *See specific types*

Slack time, 103

Spina's Fine Foods, Inc.: action steps, 160–61; action steps tie-in worksheets, 161, 163; budget, 163, 165, 166; company background, 147–48; customer/market analysis, 154; customer profile, 155; environmental analysis, 151; environmental forecast, 151–54; environmental scan, 150–51; Gantt chart, 162; internal assessment, 156, 157–58; mission, 156; objectives, 159–60; PERT chart, 164; planning process, 149–50; projected market growth, 156; standards, 163, 165–69; strategic plan, 147–69; strategic planning premises, 154, 156; strategic thrusts, 158–59

Standards, 129–31; engineering, 130–31; historical, 129–30; industry-wide standards setting, 130; legal, 130; like-group comparison, 130; Spina's Fine Foods, Inc., 163, 165–69; tie-in sheet, 131; time, 130

Strategic decision making, 7

Strategic planning: commitment to, 16, 142–43; divisional level planning, 142; elements of, 3–4; implementing process, 141–42; personnel involvement, 12–14; planning barriers, 24; plans failing list, 137–39; reasons for, 8–10; rewards from, 142–43; in uncertain environment, 10–11

Strategic planning premises, 4, 58–61; use of environmental forecast, 58; formulation of, 59–61; sample worksheet, 59; scenarios, 58–59;

Spina Fine Foods, Inc., 154, 156; worksheet, 60

Strategic planning process, 4–6; conflict resolving, 23; Spina's Fine Foods, Inc., 149–50. *See also specific processes*

Strategic thrusts, 6, 79–82; communication role, 82; definition, 79; number of, 80; use in objectives developing, 85, 90–91; use in objectives prioritizing, 94; proactive posture, 82; samples, 80–81; Spina's Fine Foods, Inc., 158–59

Survey Feedback Instrument, 65, 66, 67–68

Survey Research Center (University of Michigan), Survey Feedback Instrument, 65

Tie-in sheets, 108, 110–13; objectives-action steps sample, 115; objectives-action steps worksheet, 112–13, 114; objectives sample, 112–13; objectives worksheet, 110–11; for standards, 131; zero-based budgeting sample, 126–27

Time management, 113, 116–21; costs versus benefits comparison, 116; delegation, 122; end-point scheduling and, 102; interruptions managing, 116; meetings managing, 120; office visits managing, 120; prioritizing, 116; telephone calls managing, 119; time audit analyzing, 118; time log, 116, 117; time resource versus constraint, 116; time wasters list, 118

Tracking system: computer use, 128–29; for corrective actions, 132

Tracking system characteristics, 128–29; accuracy, 128; appropriate medium, 129; computer based, 128–29; cost effectiveness, 128; minimal duplication, 129; relevancy, 129; timeliness, 128; user language, 129. *See also* Standards

Workshops, 17–22; use in environmental analysis, 35–36; format, 17; group facilitator, 17; hidden agendas, 20–21; use in internal assessment, 63; use in objectives developing, 87; phased workshop, 19–20; planning retreat, 18–19; problems in, 20–22; short overview, 17–18

Zero-based budgeting, 124–27; sample, 126–27; worksheet, 125

About the Author

WILLIAM P. ANTHONY, Ph.D., is Professor of Management in the College of Business, Florida State University, Tallahassee. He conducts seminars, workshops, and conferences on strategic planning, managing change, participative management, and other related subjects. A frequent contributor to management and personnel journals, he has written over 40 articles and nine books, including *Participative Management, Organization Theory, Management Competencies and Incompetencies,* and the forthcoming *Managing Your Boss.*